The N
Faith-Sc
Deba

Probing Cosmology, Technology, and Theology

**Edited by
John M. Mangum**

Fortress Press ♦ Minneapolis

WCC Publications ♦ Geneva

THE NEW FAITH-SCIENCE DEBATE
Probing Cosmology, Technology, and Theology

Copyright © 1989 by Augsburg Fortress

Published by Augsburg Fortress, 426 S. Fifth St., Box 1209, Minneapolis, MN 55440 and WCC Publications, World Council of Churches, 150 route de Ferney, 1211 Geneva 2, Switzerland.

Library of Congress Cataloging-in-Publication Data

The new faith-science debate: probing cosmology,
  technology, and theology/edited by John M. Mangum.
        p.   cm.
    1. Religion and science—1946–   I. Mangum, John M.,
1920–
BL240.2.N49   1989
261.5'5—dc20   89-31708
                                                             CIP
        ISBN   0-8006-2390-8 (Fortress Press)
        ISBN   2-8254-0954-5 (WCC Publications)

Printed in the United States of America
                                                         AF 1-2390
93   92   91   90   89   1   2   3   4   5   6   7   8   9   10

✦ Contents ✦

iii

✦ Contributors ✦

Paul Abrecht is former Director of the Commission on Church and Society of the World Council of Churches, Geneva, Switzerland.

Dr. Bengt Gustafsson is Professor of Theoretical Astrophysics at the University of Uppsala, Uppsala, Sweden.

Rev. Dr. Arthur Peacocke is the former director of the Ian Ramsey Centre, St. Cross College, Oxford, England. He is an Anglican priest and for many years was a physical biochemist. He is currently Warden of the Society of Ordained Scientists.

Dr. Vítor Westhelle is Pastor of Paróquia Evangélica Luterna de Matelândia, Parana, Brazil.

Dr. Gerhard Liedke is Commissioner for Environmental Concerns of the United Evangelical Church in Baden, Federal Republic of Germany.

Dr. Harold P. Nebelsick is Professor of Doctrinal Theology at Louisville Presbyterian Seminary, Louisville, Kentucky.

Dr. Judith K. Larsen is Senior Research Scientist at Cognos Associates, Palo Alto, California.

Dr. Ronald Cole-Turner is Assistant Professor of Theology at Memphis Theological Seminary, Memphis, Tennessee.

Dr. Naozumi Eto is Assistant Professor of Systematic Theology at Japan Lutheran Theological College and Seminary, Tokyo, Japan.

Dr. Vincent P. K. Titanji is Senior Lecturer in Biochemistry and Molecular Biology at the University of Yaounde, Cameroon, West Africa.

Dr. Ted Peters is Professor of Systematic Theology at Pacific Lutheran Theological Seminary and the Graduate Theological Union, Berkeley, California.

Dr. Robert John Russell is Associate Professor of Theology and Science in Residence, the Graduate Theological Union, and Founder and Director of the Center for Theology and the Natural Sciences, Berkeley, California.

Dr. Paulos Mar Gregorios is Metropolitan of Delhi, Orthodox Syrian Church of the East, India, and a President of the World Council of Churches.

Dr. Verlyn L. Barker is Secretary for Higher Education Program and Resources for the United Church Board for Homeland Ministries, New York.

Professor Deborah Enilo Ajakaiye is Dean of Natural Sciences at the University of Jos, Nigeria.

Dr. Pradip Thomas is Assistant Professor in the Department of Communication at Tamilnadu Theological Seminary in Maduri, India.

Dr. Sigurd Martin Daecke is Professor of Systematic Theology at Rheinisch-Westfalische Technische Hochschule in the Federal Republic of Germany.

Dr. Rainer Stahl is Dozent for Old Testament Theology at the Evangelical Church Seminary in Leipzig, German Democratic Republic.

The Reverend Eric C. Shafer is Assistant to the Bishop for the Northeastern Pennsylvania Synod of the Evangelical Lutheran Church in America.

◆ Preface ◆

Seven-year-old children use computers to play video games and to solve school problems. Teen-aged students discuss "black holes" and "the big bang." Agribusiness competes in the genetic manipulation of plant life. "Co-creators" tease at eliminating "defects" in the human race. The ethics of perfecting the artificial heart for the affluent few is debated as a priority over providing basic health services for the millions of poor.

But congregations in their liturgies, pastors in their sermons, denominations in their educational programs, theologians in their publications, and seminaries in their curricula seem to live in a different world. The churches' witness often gives the impression of being designed for another place and another time, not the world of the 1990s.

Three observations about this situation are so obviously true that they should be of high priority in forming the churches' life. Tragically they seldom result in action.

One is that today's churches have no other place to fulfill their mission than a world whose basic assumptions are pervaded more and more by science.

The second is that the churches urgently need to develop strategies to communicate the gospel contextually. Society is so permeated by scientific viewpoints that when these viewpoints are not taken seriously by the churches their message is either dismissed or compartmentalized as irrelevant to serious contemporary living.

The third is that the world is flailing about in a sea of technological developments that cannot be controlled without adequate ethical guidance from the churches.

If church leaders appear uncomfortable dealing with ethical problems related to the current plethora of technology, they seem downright uneasy about engaging in serious discussion of doctrinal understandings implied by the theory of evolution and the world view of quantum physics and the theory of relativity. New understandings of human origins and human "fallenness" demand, at the very least, discussion of our understanding of God incarnate in our humanity and of the work of Jesus Christ to "restore" our "fallen" existence. "At some point," a young theologian recently said in a letter, "some church group should have the nerve to say that it cannot be business as usual anymore, not just in respect to creation, but also in respect to redemption."

In light of the churches' vocation to witness in the twentieth-century world, the Lutheran Church in America (now the Evangelical Lutheran Church in America), in cooperation with the Lutheran World Federation, sponsored a global consultation in Larnaca, Cyprus, late in 1987 with the theme, "The New Scientific/Technological World: What Difference Does It Make for the Churches?" This book is a result of that consultation. The ten essays grew out of papers that were presented there, followed by six Bible studies conducted during the conference. The group reports representing five continents are gathered in the appendices at the end of the book.

Participants were forty-five men and women still young enough to work the concern of faith/science/ethics/technology into their life agendas. (The youngest was a nineteen-year-old computer "whiz kid" from Brazil.) They came from seventeen different countries in Africa, Asia, Europe, and North and South America. While a majority were Lutheran, they ranged from Roman Catholic to Presbyterian to Anglican to Mar Thoma. They were emerging theologians and church leaders, budding scientists and technologists, and fledgling communicators.

World-class scientists, theologians, and church leaders readily agreed to give a week of their time. They made presentations, and they also mingled and chatted and dialogued with the young people. A few other persons, prominent in the faith and science discussion, were invited to round out the "International Roundtable" listed at the back of this book.

One person, absent from most sessions, made a major contribution to the consultation's success. She was Carol Seischab. She typed letters, transcribed speeches, photocopied reports, handled expense accounts, and stayed on top of the logistics of the event, including its prelude and its postlude.

The consultation is already producing results. Several participants have revised their programs of graduate study. Young Lutheran participants from the United States have organized to "lobby" the Evangelical Lutheran Church in America. Key leaders in the "International Roundtable" recently met to work toward a global network.

But the consultation will have been truly successful only when: (1) pastors preach, counsel, and lead worship in ways pertinent to the scientific/technological world in which parishioners live; (2) theologians and church leaders grapple responsibly with doctrinal questions raised by the world view of quantum physics and relativity and the theory of evolution; and (3) laypersons, in their effort to live out their Christian vocation, can make ethical decisions that have been informed by the church.

John M. Mangum

◆ Foreword ◆

Paul Abrecht

The discussion of science and faith is at least several centuries old, but the confrontation that began in the middle of this century—roughly after the discovery of nuclear energy and its use in the making of atomic bombs—has raised quite new issues.

In the earlier confrontation the fundamental issue was the clash between Christian belief and scientific knowledge, especially between the scientific understanding of the world and Christian views on creation. In that debate the churches were generally on the defensive. Eventually Christian thought recognized the contribution of science to human welfare and accepted the scientific method and the compatibility of faith and reason. By the beginning of this century Christianity had become a powerful defender of the scientific approach while resisting those scientists and theologians who tried to interpret or understand the meaning of life entirely in scientific categories.

The contemporary encounter between faith and science is quite different from the earlier one. The rapid advances of modern science, its tremendous successes, and the technological revolution to which it has led in the last half century have given rise to new concerns and questions about the future of humanity in a world increasingly dominated by scientific understanding. Today, as a result, science and science-based technology are on the defensive, and religious faith, speaking in the name of troubled and anxious humanity, has begun to ask questions about the consequences of the scientific world view. The enormous power over nature that the contemporary scientific/technological world system provides and the evident misuse of that power encourage the churches, in company with all those concerned about human welfare, to adopt a more critical stance.

This is more than failure of nerve. It is a new probing of the fundamental nature of the power that modern science/technology puts into the hands of humanity and the kind of world this produces.

It leads to a new questioning of the place of moral understanding in relation to science and technology and a new examination of the churches' critical function in relation to the scientific and technological world view. While the present confrontation began with the development of a nuclear bomb, it now extends to developments in chemistry, biology, electronics, medicine, and the space sciences, to name only a few of the areas of concern.

The churches have focused on three interrelated issues of the present crisis.

The first and most obvious is the political, economic, and social implications and consequences of rapid scientific and technological change and development. In a world where the chief criteria for national policy tend to be national security and economic advantage, and where the overriding concern is to win the commercial race to develop and exploit the new knowledge and profit from its deployment in usable consumer products (protected as "intellectual property" by a world patent system), science and technology have produced morally ambiguous results. Human welfare and happiness have been advanced for many, and no doubt critical human needs have been met. At the same time, political and economic tensions have been heightened by the race to obtain the industrial advantages and the military power science and technology make possible. As larger and larger proportions of scientific and technological research have been concentrated on military technology, undertaken by scientists and technologists whose political orthodoxy has been confirmed, both human welfare and human integrity have suffered. Moreover, the concentration of science and technology in the richer, developed countries seems likely to continue for many decades, posing questions about the meaning of justice in a world so clearly divided between the science "haves" and "have-nots."

The second dimension is the "sustainability" of a constantly growing world economic system fueled by very rapid scientific and technological development and promising ever-increasing affluence and welfare. The negative environmental consequences of such rapid economic growth and the ruthless exploitation of natural resources it has fostered, with all its uncertain side effects, have raised a host of existential, ethical, and philosophical questions about the human future for which there are as yet few convincing answers. Since so much of the pollution is global in its consequences, these are problems of great "ecumenical" interest. In this connection the discussion of "limits to growth" has raised issues, some of which have yet to be convincingly addressed, that challenge the basic assumptions of the modern consumer society. These are, however, complex and far-reaching issues and the churches have yet to show that they are ready and able to promote serious and sustained inquiry into them.

The third issue recognized by the churches concerns the need to challenge the anti-human and anti-creation assumptions inherent, if not explicit, in the modern scientific-technological world view. Despite the often repeated affirmations of scientists and technologists that their primary aim is to serve humankind, there is a growing suspicion even within the scientific community that modern science and technology are producing a distorted vision of the world, because that vision is based on philosophical assumptions contrary to the Christian understanding of humankind and its relation to the natural world. It is widely acknowledged that mechanistic, reductionist, and materialistic ideas still dominate in scientific thought and teaching. The question is, are they fundamental to the scientific world view? Leading scientists have begun to point to the human and moral consequences of the mechanistic model, which views the whole of creation as a machine. Today theologians and scientists are pressing for a review of the mechanistic approach. They are seeking to fashion a post-modern science as the first step to a post-modern world—a science based on new assumptions about God, nature, and humanity.[1]

These issues have been central in the new dialogue between the churches and the scientific community since the beginning of the ecumenical movement at Amsterdam in 1948 when Jacques Ellul first raised questions about the technical view of the world. But organized reflection on these matters only began in 1969. Subsequently they were the subject of two international World Council of Churches' conferences—one in Bucharest is 1974 and the second at the Massachusetts Institute of Technology in Boston in 1979. And they have been pursued further in the WCC and in follow-up projects like the 1987 international conference on faith and science held in Cyprus and organized by the Lutheran Church in America (now the Evangelical Lutheran Church in America) in cooperation with the Lutheran World Federation.

But these are issues that will demand persistent and continuing attention. The situation of the church in its dialogue with science is well described by Jürgen Moltmann. "They (theology and science) have become companions in tribulation under the pressure of the ecological crisis and the search for the new direction which both must work for, if human beings and nature are to survive at all on this earth." He adds, "The transition . . . is only just beginning."[2]

The essays and the discussion in this book are positive signs of the growing Christian interest and participation in the search for the new directions.

NOTES

1. See, for example, Charles Birch and John Cobb, Jr., *The Liberation of Life: From the Cell to the Community* (New York: Cambridge University Press, 1981).
2. Jürgen Moltmann, *God in Creation: A New Theology of Creation and the Spirit of God* (San Francisco: Harper & Row, 1985).

◆ I ◆

The Current Scientific World View

Bengt Gustafsson

Science is not a well-ordered, hierarchical, theoretical system. Fundamental dogmas, postulates, statements, or even results cannot be presented as basic characteristics of "a world view." Various sciences, instead, form a turmoil of different and often contradictory ideas about assumptions, methods, and results. Although tempting, it is dangerous to believe in a unified, monolithic, scientific view of the world.

If you ask a theoretical physicist for a world view, he or she probably will point to some basic but abstract concepts, or may even present some mathematical formulas as the essence. A biologist, or even an experimental physicist, on the other hand, may give you a detailed description that reminds you of the guide book to a large city. Since I am a mixture of an astronomer and a theoretical physicist, my world view will contain a little of both perspectives.

An important development in modern science is the study of complex systems with their intricate and beautiful interplay of various elements and mechanisms. Such study has to be multidisciplinary. The elaborate systems are composed of many elements traditionally studied in different branches of science. Also, a variety of research methods, often developed in separate disciplines, are used. Fields of the natural sciences that were previously rather isolated now communicate and exchange ideas and views. The investigation of complex systems that are often quite individual, with a wealth of special properties characterizing each of them, nevertheless fosters unification in science.

One example is the application of modern elementary particle physics to cosmology. In recent years the study of the largest of all

1

known structures—the universe as a whole—has been fertilized enormously by the use of new advances in particle physics. About fifteen billion years ago in the first fraction of the first second in the history of the universe, when everything was enormously compressed and hot, the most important factors governing evolution were phenomena on the smallest of all scales, the level of the elementary particle. Correspondingly, study of the universe at the astronomical perspective reveals information about the inner structure of matter at energies far beyond anything that can be reached in an earthbound accelerator as a memory of the exceedingly hot Big Bang. Together these merged fields have made possible ambitious scientific studies of such questions as: How did it all start? Could it have started differently? Why are the laws of nature as they are?

So, what is characteristic of the current scientific world view? Quantitative methods? Computer modeling? Epistemological principles? Grand unification? Or interesting examples?

Since I am a scientist I tend to point to interesting examples. To me it seems premature to take any assumed basic scientific world view too seriously. I would hesitate to base my faith in God on modern scientific studies, although contemporary science certainly demonstrates deeper insight into creation than one would previously have thought possible.

As long as scientists are active as scientists they usually do not take part in philosophical discussions. Instead, they enthusiastically describe and debate examples. They remind me of children who sit together and compare their collections of beautiful bookmarks with such things as dogs, railway engines, and angels. That activity is interesting. But writing a philosophical treatise on the aesthetics of bookmarks is not so exciting.

After looking through my own collection of bookmarks I am now, very tentatively, going to use a synthetic approach in sketching the characteristic features of current science. The selection has to be according to my own personal choice. Since it is difficult to describe such an amorphous phenomenon as current science without comparing it to something else, I shall sometimes refer to the science of the eighteenth and nineteenth centuries as a contrasting background. These comparisons will be very schematic and not intended as a genuine description of the science of previous epochs. They are just pedagogic means for discerning the properties of contemporary science more clearly.

♦ THE IMMENSE SCALES ♦

The first point I would like to make is that contemporary science has widened the scope of space and time enormously. Fifteen billion years is indeed a much more respectable age for the universe than is seven thousand years. And fifty billion light years, which is the approximate radius of the presently observable universe, is much more than the few light hours that would have been the distance to the farthest of the visible Aristotelian spheres.

These enormous abysses of space and time, opened up by modern astronomy, have correspondents in microcosm. This is clear to those who descend down to the smallest of worlds, that of the colorful quantum chromo-dynamics. The universe is characterized not only in eons of years but also in amazingly short times. A star collapses to a black hole in milliseconds. In the early phases of the universe the time intervals were so short that ordinary people today just cannot believe them.

One might object that the scientific world of the eighteenth and nineteenth centuries was even bigger, often infinite in time and space. This objection is partly valid. In particular, we are better protected against frightening infinities than was the late eighteenth-century astronomer. We have horizons in space and time and can give re-assuring answers to those who wonder what is beyond.

> *Question:* What was before the Big Bang?
> *Answer:* Space-time did not exist. There was no time, so the very word "before" would have been meaningless.
> *Question:* Is the universe infinite?
> *Answer:* We cannot tell directly since light is emitted from regions so distant that its travel time exceeds the age of the universe. That light could not have reached us yet. All we can see, in principle, are the contents of a huge sphere around us. We are in the center of that sphere, which is about 100 billion light years across.

Even around the frightening black holes, which are local infinities in space-time itself, there are protecting horizons. We do not have to see them.

Nevertheless I claim that our world is more extensive than the infinite world of the nineteenth-century astronomer. We have new, wonderful worlds with qualitatively and quantitatively new properties for each step up or down the space-time ladder. The nineteenth-century astronomer's world just boringly repeated itself to infinity.

◆ THE ABSTRACT NATURE OF FUNDAMENTALS ◆

My next point is that when new worlds in new scales are studied a number of fundamental concepts that were taken for granted are found to be invalid, or at least not very useful. To replace them, more abstract, fundamental concepts must be constructed.

A standard example is the conceptualization of waves and particles. When these concepts are used to describe matter in microcosmos, odd absurdities result. To overcome these absurdities, a more useful but also much more abstract concept—the wave function—has been constructed. Several years of training as a physicist are needed before you can picture that concept. And actual experiments give you only partial information about the properties of a wave function. In addition, the wave function is severely deformed or destroyed by your attempts to measure it.

Another example of the problems connected to our use in science of concepts from everyday life is the conceptualization of space and time. Space and time are different for different observers, depending on their relative motion and the strengths of the gravitational field. This astonishing result from the theory of relativity is very well anchored in modern high-precision experiments. And its consequences are far-reaching.

If you unfortunately fell into the enormously strong gravitational field of a black hole, I would see you moving more and more slowly, like an unusually dull sloth. Even the hands on your watch would rotate very slowly. I would receive less and less light from you, and soon I would not see you at all.

Your experience would be more remarkable and more interesting. You would see me moving around rapidly, as in a film from the early twentieth century. You would see me die, and you could wave your hands to my grandchildren's grandchildren. Before you got started, however, they would be dead. After five billion years you would see the sun die. The stars would tend to concentrate above your head, for under you would lie the black hole. Long before you had completed this interesting experience, I fear, your body would have been pulled out into a long, thin thread because the enormously strong gravitational field would have more force on your feet than on your head (provided you fell with your feet toward the hole, which I would do if I were you). Space and time would not behave as in our living rooms where we do not move rapidly in relation to each other and where we do not sit in strong gravitational fields.

A more basic, and more useful, concept is that of four-dimensional space-time. This concept allows time to be transformed into space and vice versa, depending on the distribution of motion and matter.

Interesting efforts have been made by James Hartle and Steven Hawking toward discovering the initial characteristics of the Big Bang. The problem is to define a simple and natural beginning of the universe that could still give rise to our seemingly special world. In the first billionth of a billionth of a billionth of a billionth of a second, during the most remarkably compact stages of matter, quantum effects dominate the behavior of the universe as a whole. Under these extreme conditions time seems much more space-like. Instead of time and three-dimensional space, we find something with the properties of a four-dimensional space only.

Hartle and Hawking have proposed a simple and more natural geometry and topology of this four-dimensional space. They suggest it to be that of a sphere, or better, a hemisphere. On the surface of a sphere there is no preferential point, no place where the sphere begins. So the question of the beginning of the universe seems dissolved, or at least swept under the rug. Time as we know it did not exist then. It appeared, more or less gradually, from a space without any special edge or event.

This work of Hartle and Hawking has a somewhat *ad hoc* character. And it brings the warning that one should not put too much literal emphasis on the very beginning. If we localize a creator there, that creator may vanish into the beginning himself.

While discussing difficult matters I want to mention the work by several groups on rotating universes, and particularly the work of the team headed by Bertel Laurent in Stockholm. It is well recognized that all known objects in the universe rotate. It is also quite possible that the universe as a whole is rotating, though very slowly. (You could certainly ask, "Rotating relative to what?" But that question can be answered satisfactorily.)

If all the universe is rotating, it seems possible to make unusual journeys. Should you take an immense trip through billions of years, using considerable but still finite amounts of fuel, at the end you or your descendants would return to the earth before you left. So imagine that you are preparing for takeoff in your gigantic space ship. You are testing the refrigeration chest where you are to sleep for millions of centuries when an old man totters up to you. He tells you that he is you in an elderly edition, and he begs you not to start this journey. What will happen if you obey him?

This paradox, breaking causality, may lead to the conclusion that the universe does not rotate, or alternatively, that causality is one of those primitive, seemingly fundamental concepts that must be dethroned eventually.

I shall summarize this second point with a 1930 quotation of Paul Dirac.

"The classical tradition," Dirac wrote, "has been to regard the world as a collection of observable objects (particles, fluids, fields, and so forth) that move according to certain definitive laws for the natural forces, so that a picture can be made of the full scheme, in space and time. But it has become clear in recent years that nature works on a different level. Its fundamental laws do not govern in a very direct way the world as we see it. Instead, they control a level of which we cannot make a concrete picture without introducing contradictions."

♦ THE EVER-GROWING COMPLEXITY ♦

My third point has been alluded to in my introduction. It is that our world is much more complex than it was before. Atoms, for instance, were small, hard balls in those days. Now they are worlds, enormously rich in complexity, displaying the fantastic possibilities of quantum mechanics and quantum chromodynamics. Many of these phenomena are not well understood. Moreover, our atoms have a fantastic cosmic origin in dying stars, exploding long before the material for the solar system was assembled.

Cells used to be the simple building blocks in organic materials. Now each of them is a more intricate universe than all of nature was to a scientist two centuries ago. I know a person who has devoted her life to the study of a particular one-cell organism. Her compassion for, almost solidarity with, these fantastic beings is admirable and fully understandable.

Grayish slime or mucus in the human body is now viewed as whole societies with interaction among many different actors. Transport systems carry goods and waste, and communication systems carry signals—flexible, logical networks with a high degree of sophistication.

One of my most frustrating experiences was at a conference for pastors. After my talk one after another said in varying ways, "This is very nice. But, after all, a human cannot be only a naked ape."

Only a naked ape!

You should be grateful if you were an atomic nucleus. You ought to praise the Lord if you were a living cell. A naked ape is something enormously fine that none of us could ever deserve to be!

An interesting apparent paradox is connected with the growth of this complicated picture of an expanding universe where matter and radiation continually disperse and the second law of thermodynamics rules, where it would seem that disorder instead of order should increase. I suppose that any scientist, if he or she had not recognized that it was our universe in its youth, would not give the conditions in an almost uniform, hot, expanding gas much of a chance to form galaxies, stars, heavy atomic nuclei, planetary systems, and life. "If there were no stars up there," one astronomer said, "it would be simple to prove that there cannot be any stars up there."

Where does all of this structure come from?

This is a lively field of research today. It involves studies of collective processes far from equilibrium, of so-called self-organizing systems, of the unexpected structure of systems approaching chaos, of non-linear differential equations, of neural networks and information theory. We do not know what will come out of all of this. One hope is that we shall find a fairly general theory describing the growth and the conditions for growth of complex structures.

Until such a theory has been found we cannot tell if all this structure was safely inherent in the beginning of the universe, like the lily in the bulb. There could have been critical points in the history of the universe on which the realization of this structure totally depended.

My hope is that eventually even the formation of the beautiful inherent structure reflected in our laws of nature will be understood as part of a scientific description of the history of the universe. But we are far from that goal.

Another line of thought, known as "the anthropic principle," is discussed in this connection from time to time. It points in a rather different direction regarding "why the laws of nature are as they are." The basis for the anthropic principle is the observation that the intricate chain of events—from the Big Bang to the formation of galaxies, of stars, of such heavy atomic nuclei as carbon, of life—is very fragile in regard to small disturbances in the laws and forces of nature. For instance, if you postulate that the strong nuclear force that keeps nuclei together had been stronger or weaker by a small percentage, the whole delicate chain would have burst. Life would have been much more difficult, even for stars. We seem to live in an optimal universe, optimal for most complex structures that we can imagine. This observation has led to the metaphysical hypothesis that our universe is just one in an infinite ensemble of worlds with different properties and laws of nature.

There are several objections against the anthropic principle, as well as against the many worlds hypothesis. The principle is systematically based on *ad-posteriori* evidence. It has not contributed much in understanding. It seems weak in predictive power. It may also devalue the ambition of scientific explanations to a bunch of just-so stories.

On the other hand, there is also support for these hypotheses. They could well mark the beginning of a new (or renewed) and different view of the possibilities of scientific explanation. Seemingly teleological explanations could then be given to many questions, explanations that relate to our existence as one of the most characteristic properties of our universe. It seems fair that the word *anthropos* has been used in naming the principle. It would certainly bring humankind to a central position in the understanding of nature. Although we would not be the masters of creation, we would certainly be its darlings.

"What really interests me," Einstein said, "is whether God had any choice when he created the world."

♦ THE BEAUTIFUL SCIENCE ♦

Through Einstein, I now come to my fourth and last point. It is about beauty. The importance of aesthetic arguments in contemporary theoretical physics is amazing. Einstein's work is one of the best examples. One does not exaggerate when one says that striving for beauty and internal consistency led to the theory of general relativity. This would not be so amazing if the theory were mainly a systematic way of summarizing old experiments and observations. But it was not. It was certainly effective in this respect, but its genius was that it was able to lead to highly spectacular and almost unbelievable predictions of very odd phenomena. These predictions have been verified.

Another example is the work of the great physicist Hermann Weyl. "In my work I always try to combine truth with beauty," he stated, "but when I must choose between them I prefer beauty." Later he was asked by one of his students if he could give an example of a theory he had kept alive because of its beauty although it was wrong. He then mentioned his theory of gravitation, which certainly was wrong. Two decades later, however, after Weyl was dead, this theory was used by others in unifying forces of nature other than gravitation.

In fact, many of the leading theoretical physicists in this century have confessed the importance of aesthetic criteria in their work. They have told of the joy they experienced when they found solutions still more beautiful than they had thought possible. It is admittedly difficult to communicate the character of mathematical beauty. Symmetry and uniformity play a role, but so do broken symmetrics and bizarre aberrations. Few studies in the aesthetics of science have been carried out, and we do not understand why aesthetic criteria have proven so successful in recent decades.

♦ FINAL REMARKS ♦

So here are the four characteristics of my collection of scientific bookmarks: the immense scale and scope, the abstract nature of fundamentals, the ever-growing complexity, and the beauty.

Other characteristics could have been chosen instead: the imperialistically expanding dominance of science into all regions of culture and thought, the childish belief that all knowledge is good in the long run, the constant and sometimes deliberate confusion between over-simplified models and reality, or the commercial interests behind what I fear has become the religion of our time—belief in science.

Science as a religion may seem advanced and sophisticated to some people. Personally I do not think it is. I wonder if it is not primarily an old shamanism reappearing in a vacuum. Look at the scientist on TV traveling to the ends of the universe, or to the innermost of the atoms, or to the first appearance of *homo sapiens*. To his TV parish he brings news about what really matters, while the nearby "ordinary world" may seem trivial and unimportant. Yet the scientist confidently offers advice about everything.

That is why I say, "Don't take science too seriously." Its consequences are too serious for that. Sometimes, even often, you may rely on scientific statements about the world. But do not believe in science itself. In particular, do not rely on science as a solution to societal, relational, personal, or existential problems. You may well use it, but do not rely on it. The scientific world view is impressive and even important but not sufficient. There are also solutions other than scientific solutions.

·2·

The Challenge of Science to Theology and the Church

Arthur Peacocke

My intention is to reflect on the images and models of Christian theology in the light of our understanding of the natural world gained from the sciences.

In doing this I in no sense repudiate the past for I am constantly encouraged by what rich treasures lie buried in the history of the Christian church waiting to be rediscovered.

I am convinced, though, that the most vital theology of the church has always been hammered out in response to new intellectual confrontations and to new social and political pressures. I recall the great contribution of the Cappadocian Fathers, who met the challenge of Greek philosophy. I recall the conflicts that led to the creeds and affirmations of the early church councils. I recall St. Thomas Aquinas who, despite much opposition, refashioned Christian theology after the influx of Aristotle's writings. He did his work so well that it lasted until quite recently, when it too became a straitjacket.

The presuppositions of what I say will be critically realist with respect to both science and theology. I believe that both science and theology aim to depict reality. I believe that they both do so with metaphorical language, which is revisable, and I believe that they do so in the context of continuous linguistic communities.

We have to take seriously the broad features of the history of the natural order that is afforded by the sciences. We should not, however, take some recent speculations too seriously. A theology that marries the science of today may well be a widow tomorrow. Even so, some features of the world have become so well established that we would be foolish not to take account of them. It is true that human beings make mistakes, but there is no virtue in believing that they make nothing but mistakes. Theology simply must deal with some features of the world that have emerged from the scientific endeavors of the last three centuries.

The resources for our theology continue, of course, to be Scripture and tradition, ways God has spoken in the past through the frameworks of thought of the past. Today we still wish to refer to the activity of God in Christ through the Holy Spirit, yet we must do so with the means provided by our own frameworks of thought if we wish to be understood by our contemporaries. God is still actively revealing, and the new wine of today needs new wineskins.

We need to apply our reason to our resources—the Bible, the tradition, and our experience, which includes a new awareness of the world through the natural sciences. We seek intelligibility, intellectual coherence, and meaning for ourselves as individuals in our brief sojourn in God's created order. The contemporary person needs to hear the Word that is eternally uttered by the Creator to his creation in a language that he or she can understand and respond to. Today one of the universal languages of humanity cutting across all cultural boundaries is that of science.

I am going to take some of the "heads" of Christian doctrine and see what images and metaphors and language might be used in thinking about them, and I shall do so in the light of the broadest and best established features of the scientific picture of the world. I apologize for the somewhat stark brevity of my treatment enforced by the limitations of our discourse here.

◆ GOD ◆

The first such "head," of course, is God. The primary attribute of God in the monotheistic religions is *transcendence* over the world, over all-that-is. We recognize immediately that the totality of all-that-is is not self-explanatory. Even the original quantum fluctuation had to have some mode of being of a kind to which quantum mechanics could specifically apply. The affirmation of the existence and transcendence of God is a response to the question of why there is anything at all.

I am taking this affirmation of the transcendence of God as a premise in everything that follows. From this understanding we derive the sense of God as creator, as giving being to all-that-is. God is the ground of all being, Being itself—while the world has derived and dependent being. This is one of the fundamental pillars of Christian theology, and of all the monotheistic religions.

The givenness of the parameters and laws of the universe has been re-emphasized recently in the "anthropic principle": this universe is characterized by a particular set of laws and fundamental constants that have the inherent property of allowing the development of life and living matter and so of ourselves. The anthropic principle re-emphasizes, from a theological viewpoint, the contingency of all-that-is. It could have been otherwise. It need not have been at all in the form it was. So the anthropic principle contributes a new nuance to our understanding of God's transcendence and to the contingency of our own existence.

In twentieth-century physics there has been a development, stemming from Einstein, in which the categories of space and time, which seemed so given and *a priori* to Kant, are themselves fused together. They are conceived in a new kind of synthesis because space, time, matter, and energy have become interlocking concepts that physicists cannot readily separate. We now have to talk about four-dimensional space-time. But space-time, matter, and energy are interlocked, for the curvature of space-time is related to the gravitational field that is, of course, related to the concept of mass, and so on.

Any idea that God gives being to all-that-is must include time, as Augustine and the Fathers knew. God is, in some sense, the creator *of* time. The doctrine of creation is not, in the first instance, a statement about what happened "in" space-time. Space-time, matter, and energy are all aspects of the created order. God has to be regarded as other than, and transcending, space-time, matter, and energy. The doctrine of creation is fundamentally about the relation of God to all-that-is, and this refers to space-time-matter-energy. So modern physics has reemphasized a fundamental insight of theology going back to Augustine and even earlier.

There is in modern physics a great mystery in our understanding of matter, energy, space, and time. The world is very mysterious in its ultimate depths. It is also mysterious in its ultimate heights. There is a real mystery about the nature of human personhood, both as we perceive it within ourselves and in our relations to each other. Science has not dispelled the ultimate mystery about the nature of matter and of the self. This points to the inevitable mystery of God's own being. The transcendence of God is enriched by the perspectives the sciences now give us.

We have, I think, a further clue in that self-transcendence we have over our bodies. We are immanent in our bodies and we act in them as they obey the laws of nature. Here, perhaps, is a model for the transcendence of God over a world that is increasingly intelligible to the sciences.

Another classical feature of the God of Christian truth is that of the *immanence* of God in the world. So let us look at how the world appears to the sciences today. We observe natural processes that are continuous and inherently creative. Matter has the ability to be self-organizing into new forms. The process is open-ended, and the details of the process are often unpredictable in principle. They occur by the interplay of what we call "chance" and law. Though not strictly always predictable, they are often intelligible *post hoc*. There seems to be an inbuilt tendency in matter, and in the processes it undergoes, towards complexity, awareness, information transfer, and, ultimately, consciousness, cognition, and self-consciousness. Potentialities appear to be being actualized. The original "Hot Big Bang," with its cloud of neutrinos, quarks, or whatever, has become *us*. Nature not only has, but *is* a history of events. There seems to be no inert stuff. All is constituted by events, by "goings-on." The universe manifests emergence of the genuinely new. This genuinely new has to be discussed in language that is not entirely reducible to the languages pertinent to that from which the new has emerged.

If we are to think of God as creator of such a universe, we must re-emphasize that God is still creating "in, with, and under" the processes of the natural world all the time. God is *semper Creator.* The world is a *creatio continua.* God as creator, in this view, not only sustains the world (the classical view) but is regarded as continuously creating in and through its processes to bring forth the new. God is in, with, and under the creative processes.

I deliberately use sacramental language here. God must be understood as exploring and actualizing the potentialities of creation, achieving ends flexibly, knowing the general direction and not fixing the historical process in advance. God is improvising rather as Bach did before the king of Prussia, making his "musical offering," or perhaps as a New Orleans jazz player would extemporize. Creating is the action of God the composer at work.

The processes of creation appear to be open-ended. There is increasing individuality of organisms as one goes up the biological scale, culminating in the freedom of *homo sapiens.* It seems that God, as Creator, self-limits his omniscience by allowing openness and flexibility and freedom to emerge.

We also see, through our scientific spectacles, that death is the precondition of new life. Consciousness, and so awareness, cannot evolve without the development of nervous systems and other recording devices that are able to react negatively to their environment with what we call pain. It appears that pain and suffering are the precondition of sensitivity and consciousness, and that death of the individual organism is the precondition for new forms of life to appear. What theologians used to call "natural evil" now seems to be a necessary part of the process for the production of new life and consciousness.

What do we make of a God who works through such a process? It can only become acceptable if we regard God as suffering in, with, and under the creative processes of the world. God is enduring what we call "natural evil" for the ultimate good and fruition of what is being created.

The world also shows an enormous fecundity and diversity in its organic life. Science can demonstrate that an extraordinary unity underlies this diversity, and that the operation of relatively simple principles has led to this amazing variety. We cannot assume that all this marvelous, rich life is there simply in order that some chance flick of the genes will produce human beings at some point. God must be assumed to have joy in the creative order in its own right, in its own vitalities, at its own levels, and for its own sake. (Here, incidentally, we might have the basis for a more theo-centric ecological ethic.) God must be assumed to delight in the existence of all forms of life and not only in *homo sapiens,* although God can delight in human beings too. (Psalm 104 is a marvelous expression of God's delight in *all* of creation.)

So, where are we? God's immanence in the creating process has to be re-affirmed and re-emphasized in light of the sciences. For three or four centuries the emphasis on God's immanence has gone underground. We must bring it to the surface again.

In some sense the world is "in" God, yet God is "more than" the world. God in this image is rather Creator-Mother than Creator-Father. God gives new forms and life to what is in "her." The ultimate being of God, of course, is other than space, time, matter, energy. But when we say the world is "in" God, the preposition "in" here is a spatial metaphor. We are trying to say that there is a projection of God into a dimension of reality lower than, or within, him or herself.

There is still in all this, and it has been perennial in Christian theology, a tension between transcendence and immanence. We very much need a model to bring these two ideas, distinct though they are, into some kind of overlapping focus of transcendence-in-immanence. I think we can begin to see such a model in our own human experience. We are self-transcendent in our consciousness over our bodies, yet there is a sense that we are ourselves immanent in and through our bodies. Perhaps this is one of the multiple senses, discussed in Christian history, in which we are *imago dei.* If this is so, then perhaps the truest image, or *icon,* we have of God is through a human person who is fully open to God. That person is, so to speak, transparent to the divine life and being—embodying that self-limitation of omniscience and of omnipotence which is a ramification of God's Being of Love itself. There is a kind of self-emptying (a *kenosis*) of God in creation that calls for explicit manifestation.

This modality of God as Creator also points to the self-expression of God's own inherent being as creative love—acting on behalf of the coming into existence and flourishing of something other than God, the created order. Our language always falls short of depicting such a reality. We have to say that God is "at least personal" and it then becomes legitimate to think of God as self-communicating through creation, as the prologue of St. John's Gospel informs us. That prologue also reminds us that any meanings God intended to communicate through God's Word uttered in creation are uttered to creatures capable of discerning them.

This has certain consequences. Different meanings of God are communicated at the different levels of creation according to the capacity of those levels to receive the information, the message, the meaning of God. So if we say that God is "at least personal," can we not hope that in a person, or persons, sometime, some place, God might unveil his meaning, express his/her word in a fullness appropriate to our human capacity to discern and respond to it?

This brings us to a consideration of our presence in the world and to the significance and potentiality of human being.

◆ HUMAN NATURE ◆

In the perspective of the sciences we see human beings as psychosomatic unities, evolving by natural processes, emerging into consciousness and self-consciousness with freedom in community. There seems to be a continuous evolution to the vertebrates and to the higher primates. Then in *homo sapiens* special features appear that are not entirely discontinuous with those of his and her predecessors—a highly developed brain, flexibility, use of language, social cooperation. But in human beings a certain incandescent mix of these qualities becomes manifest. The activity of the human-brain-in-the-human-body displays qualities to which we have to apply new non-reducible language. Human unity is not that of a body plus a "mind" plus a "soul." "Persons" possess a unity which emerges from a continuous history, but which is, nevertheless, genuinely new. I do not need to remind those of you who are students of the Bible that this emphasis on the psychosomatic unity of the human being squares very well with the biblical view of the human being in both the Old and New Testaments.

A second feature of human nature we must recognize is the biological death of the individual. We as individuals would not be here at all if our predecessors had not undergone biological death. So when St. Paul says that "the wages of sin is death," that cannot possibly mean for us, now, *biological* death. Biological death was present on the earth long before human beings arrived. It is the prerequisite of our coming into existence through the creative processes of biology which God himself has installed in the world. So in that phrase St. Paul can only, for us, mean "death" in some figurative sense of, [perhaps], the death of our relationship to God as the consequence of sin. I cannot see any sense in regarding biological death as the consequence of our alienation from God, because God had already made biological death the means of his creating new forms of life. This has to be accepted, difficult though it may be for some theologies.

Another feature of the emergence of human nature is the continuity of the process. There seems to be no break of any substantial kind in the sequence observed by paleontologists and anthropologists. There is no past period of moral perfection. There is no evidence that human society was once a perfect society from which it later declined. All the evidence points to a creature emerging into awareness, with an increasing capacity for consciousness and sensitivity and, ultimately, the possibility of moral responsibility and response to God.

But always the creature that emerges seems not to be fully formed. It is, as it were, "on the way," with increasing aspirations, increasing possibilities of both exaltation and degradation as human powers over nature increase. Self-consciousness, *ipso facto,* makes humanity aware of its limitations and of its failures to fulfill its aspirations. Humanity now shapes its own evolution, and evolution has become psychosocial and internalized and self-directing. In fact, it has become "history."

So there is no sense in which we can talk of a "fall" from a past perfection. There was no golden age, no perfect past, no perfect individual "Adam" from whom human beings have now descended. Humanity manifests only aspirations to perfection yet to be attained, potentiality yet to be actualized, and no "original righteousness." Sin, which is real, is about a falling short of what God intends us to be and is concomitant with our possession of self-consciousness, freedom, and intellectual curiosity. This seems to me to be a theological interpretation of sin that could make sense to our contemporaries.

We have an awareness of the tragedy of our failure to fulfill our aspirations, of our failure to come to terms with finitude, death, and suffering, of our failure to realize our potentialities and to steer our path through life. All of these are realities of the human situation. Freedom allows us the choice to make the wrong choices. Sin and alienation from God and from humanity are real features of our existence. But our theology will be going along the wrong track if it is based on presuppositions of an ideal past from which we have fallen. Humanity emerges into consciousness and then comes into awareness, language, a sense of moral responsibility, and an understanding of truth, beauty, and goodness—and the freedom to do evil.

As this self-consciousness comes into existence the possible fluctuations about any norm get bigger and bigger. Human beings become capable of greater heights and greater degradation than any other animal. With the emergence of self-awareness, *homo sapiens* has the opportunity of *both* higher achievement and greater debasement.

Within the processes of creation there has come into existence a being capable of self-transcendence, an "I" that knows itself over against its own body in the natural world and thinks of itself as a subject. This human being has emerged within nature by natural processes which, by and large, the sciences now render intelligible. Does this not raise the hope that the immanence of God in that part of the natural order which is humanity might perhaps display a "broken image" of the transcendence as well as the immanence of God? Because God has produced this being in and through the process, the transcendence and immanence of human consciousness and bodily experience raises the conjecture that in humanity the immanence of God might one day display, in a unique and newly emergent manner, a transcendent dimension to a degree that would unveil without distortion the transcendent-Creator-who-is-immanent.

But humanity is only a broken and distorted image of God. Human beings have misused their freedom by putting themselves at the center of their lives and their universe. "You will be like God," said the Tempter (Gen. 3:5). Suppose, however, that a human being freely chose to be so open to God's immanent presence in the world that his/her life was totally God-centered. Would not that be the ultimate unveiling of God's being, mode of becoming, and meaning for the discernment and response of humanity? Would it not then be accurate to say that, in such a person, the immanence of God had displayed a transcendent dimension to such a degree that the presence of God in that actual psychosomatic personal unity required new non-reducible concepts to express a unique transcendence in and through immanence (in fact, the concept of "incarnation")?

♦ HUMANITY EVOLVED AND GOD INCARNATE ♦

In our consideration of evolved humanity we have come very close to the idea that God was incarnate in a human person. For we are among those who believe that this manifestation of God as transcendence-in-immanence has actually happened in history in the person of Jesus the Christ. Why we believe this and what evidence we have adduced to affirm that in this person God has uniquely unveiled the mystery of his being is a matter for other occasions.

Even so, we still have to ask what is the significance of the life, death, and resurrection of Jesus for humanity in its search today for God's meaning in a created order that is increasingly described and rendered intelligible by the natural sciences. Various aspects, some of them very tentative, of how God as Creator relates to the created order can now be picked out of my earlier remarks and re-considered in the light of Christian belief.

If God is actually creating through the kind of processes we see in the sciences, then God must in some sense be regarded as self-offering and suffering love active in creation. This is entirely coherent with a recognition of Jesus the Christ's self-offering in suffering love. On the cross we have a fuller revelation of God's *own* love in suffering to create.

I also talked about God's conveying his, or her, meaning through the personal and through the different levels of the created order. I suggested that God's meaning might be more fully made clear— God's message and "informing" might be transferred more fully— through the level of that unique entity, the "person." This comes very close to a doctrine of the incarnation. Jesus' openness to God, in this perspective, leads to our discernment of God's presence in action in Jesus. We would have to regard "incarnation" as the word for that new emergent non-reducible concept applicable to this unique person, Jesus of Nazareth, who is the manifestation of God's transcendence immanent in a human life. God's immanence-in-transcendence shines through the image of the person of Jesus, being the perfect vehicle for conveying to us what the transcendence and immanence of God might be.

I described the processes in the natural world as emergent, open-ended, and continuous. Jesus was fully open to God and obedient to God. He was one with the ever-acting God who brings forth the new in the created order. He was one with God's work in the world, one with initiating God's reign over all. By virtue of his openness to God as his Father *(Abba)* and Creator, Jesus was able to express with unique originality the transcendence of the Creator immanent in the world process.

I am here concerned not so much with Jesus' nature or what kind of substances do, or did, constitute him (the terrain of the classical debate of the first five centuries of the church), but rather with the dynamic nature of the relation between God's immanent creative *activity,* focused and unveiled in him, and the *processes* of nature, of human history and experience. There is an activity of God going on all the time that is peculiarly and manifestly focused in the personal life of this Jesus of Nazareth.

I talked about God unveiling his meaning in various and distinctive levels. In this perspective, Jesus the Christ mediates to us the meaning of creation—at least that strand leading to self-conscious personal life. As Emil Brunner once put it, "The love of God is the *causa finalis* of the creation. In Jesus Christ this ideal reason for creation is revealed." The meaning which God communicates through the life, death, and resurrection of Jesus is the meaning God wants to communicate both *about* humanity and *for* humanity. In Jesus the meaning he (Jesus) discerns, proclaims, expresses, and reveals is the meaning that he himself *is*.

We begin to see the first great chapter of St. John's Gospel in a new light. We see that there the Word, the Logos of God, the Word uttered in creation, is dispersed throughout creation. It is perennial, general, implicit, but incognito. With the incarnation in the person of Jesus this activity and presence of God immanent in creation becomes focused, historic, particular, explicit, manifest. All this is summed up in the Johannine literature, as well as in the New English Bible translation of 1 John 1: "It was there from the beginning; we have heard it; we have seen it with our own eyes; we looked upon it and felt it with our hands: and it is of this we tell. Our theme is the word of life. This life was made visible. . . ."

This is a perspective in which we can see the significance of the incarnation, the expression of God in Jesus, as both continuous with what went before and as a genuinely new emergent requiring all the special language of "incarnation" that the church has applied to that unique event. But this uniqueness, you will notice, is potentially a generality. This evolutionary perspective allows us both to recognize the continuity of Jesus with us—he was a human being—and the distinctiveness. The evolutionary process all the time shows emergence out of the old into the new. New forms come into existence that require new concepts and language for expressing their uniqueness and distinctiveness. So we can accept both the continuing and the emergence, both the immanence of God in the creative process and the incarnation in the sense of a specific and explicit manifestation of God in a unique way. In this sense Christ is the consummation of the evolution of the creative work of love in the whole process.

What does this mean about the "work of Christ," as the theologians call it?

♦ THE WORK OF CHRIST ♦

All of the foregoing gives a vantage point from which we can now view the redemptive work of Christ in a new perspective. It has the consequence that what happened to Jesus could in principle happen to all of humanity. God can be incarnate in us to the extent to which we open our total selves to God and freely respond to do his will. When we do this we, in a Pauline phrase, "take the shape of Christ" (Gal. 4:19). Or, again as St. Paul said, "We are transfigured into his likeness" (2 Cor. 3:17). We become what God intended us to be.

Christ is indeed the "second Adam," even if the first was only an invention of our hopes for perfection. He is the "second Adam" because he is the primal ancestor of the new humanity that truly "images" God. This is, of course, the whole theme of "deification," "divinization," *"theosis"* that the Fathers emphasized.

I would like us to get back to that strand in Christian theology I associate particularly with Irenaeus. In a great phrase he said, "Our Lord Jesus Christ, the Word of God, of his boundless love became what we are that he might make us what he himself is." This seems to me a positive understanding of redemption. Now, instead of simply being a reversal of a past collapse, it takes on a positive dynamic view as the means whereby God is creating a new humanity through the work of God in Christ through the Holy Spirit. It is not the restoring of a *past* original perfection, that of a mythical first Adam, but an initiative of God that raises humanity into the life of God. Christ is the forerunner of a new possibility for human existence. This possibility is made actual through Christ's human response of obedience and openness, which was in itself an initiative of God as Holy Spirit immanent within the created order. Humanity now knows it can live its life in and with God. That is our destiny and our hope.

So "redemption from sin" is no longer some rather abstruse transaction within the divine in which a change of mind is induced in God. It is, rather, a manifestation of God's perennial loving, gracious intention to actualize our God-given potentialities of personhood by bringing humanity into his own life through God's own self-offering and suffering love rekindled in us. It is a path costly to God and costly to us.

It seems to me that this understanding of redemption and sanctification is wholly cognate and congruent with both the Christian revelation and an evolutionary and scientific perspective. It gives the Christian faith a way to communicate with a generation to whom the old language based on those other images is often totally incomprehensible and unbelievable. Those who have been nurtured in the bosom of the church and fed on its Scriptures may well have so made the traditional images their own that they are natural to and true for them. But for ninety percent of our contemporaries, that language is totally mystifying and incomprehensible.

I am simply suggesting a way in which we might, true to Christian insights and close to many strands in the Christian tradition, talk about salvation in a believable manner. Salvation is about making whole—about health, wholeness, wholesomeness. It is about living our life in and with God. It is about being taken into the presence of God and being reshaped after the image of Christ so that God creates, as it were, Christ within us and we become one with the resurrected Jesus the Christ. It makes intelligible how what happened in and to Jesus *then* can have significance for us *now.*

Consistent with this perspective, the following themes might be identified for further development.

The church could be regarded as the community of those who, through God in Christ through the Holy Spirit, are becoming one with God. In them the creative act of God in evolution is being brought to fulfillment in community through the creation of a new modality of human existence. (A new "species?") The doctrine of the church should deal with the new possibilities for human togetherness in society. These basically New Testament concepts could have a new dimension today in this context of continuity with evolution.

Matter itself also takes on a new meaning. In the evolutionary perspective we have to realize that matter is not what we thought it was when we talked about it in terms of Newtonian billiard balls, as atoms in the periodic table, or even in terms of quantum physics. We now know that through the evolutionary process matter becomes persons. Break us all down and we are just a pile of hydrogen, carbon, nitrogen, oxygen, iron, phosphorus, and other atoms. But we are also persons. In us matter has become persons. There is no division between us and the matter of which we are made. Matter in the form of us becomes persons who know God and who worship.

Such an insight into the potentialities of matter has been continuously preserved in the church by its sacramental language. When Jesus at the Last Supper said, "This my body, this my blood," and pointed to things of the created order—bread and wine made by persons out of the elements of nature—he was giving a new value and a new meaning to the stuff of the universe. The sacramental tradition of the church has mercifully preserved in its liturgy the utter seriousness and significance with which we must regard the stuff of the universe. This is now very consonant with our understanding of how the stuff of the world is in fact the matrix of personality, that which becomes persons. The created world itself is a kind of sacrament.

◆ CONCLUSION ◆

If the foregoing has any weight, then it seems to me the church must rethink its message in today's language for any scientifically educated society. That does not mean only the so-called "First World." Increasingly scientific education, an understanding of the natural history of the world, has become spread throughout all cultures. The old images, although they are meaningful to those brought up in the bosom of the church, no longer sound at all credible to those outside. We need a rebirth of images in continuity with what we have received from the Scriptures and tradition by revising how we speak of the eternal realities and verities to which we want to refer, to which we wish to point. We must rethink our metaphors and our language. We need a recovery of credibility and plausibility in the content of the church's message, and this will take time.

The importance of *ideas* here cannot be underestimated. It is our duty to interpret the meanings of the person of Jesus and of his actions in ways intelligible to our contemporaries. That means we have got to take into our Christian reflection some of those features of the natural world about which I have been talking. Theologians who make no reference to the scientific picture of the world are just digging themselves into a deeper and deeper hole, and, as they go down, they will be able only to talk more and more to themselves and less and less to other people. We must talk to our contemporaries, and to ourselves, in language—models and metaphors—that are meaningful in the world we increasingly are coming to know: that of the sciences.

·3·

The Challenge of Theology to Science and the Church

Vítor Westhelle

Theology is a provisional enterprise. I do not mean that only in a temporal sense, in the sense that it will be surpassed in time. I mean provisional also in a spacial sense. Theology is provisional in that it is determined by the lives, the dreams, the words, and the deeds of people experiencing displacement but sharing the faith that God's love will not fail.

I think of marking points in our tradition: Sarah and Abraham in their migration, searching for a promised land. Slaves in Egypt going out because God has heard their cry. Widows, orphans, and dispossessed whose voices were raised by Nathan, by Elijah, by Amos, and by Isaiah. I think of Jeremiah and Job. Of second Isaiah's word of comfort and encouragement to a people living in exile. I think of Mary's song, of the child without a place to be born, of the boy raised in Nazareth from which nothing good could come. I think of the man who, not having a place to lay his head, became a neighbor to all who live in the same condition.

I think of the people in this world who are hanging by their nails in the abyss of displacement. Particularly now I think of the women and men in Latin America, in Africa, in Asia, in Europe, in the United States who live without a place.

So I speak from my own situation. I could not do otherwise. I speak from the places I know and from the places in which I participate. One can be universal only by being radically particular. It is in particular situations that theology raises its voice. And these situations are where the struggle of life and death is being fought.

This is the concern of theology: life in concrete circumstances where time dissipates itself due to the lack of a place.

Let me share with you the words of Carolina Maria de Jesus, a woman living in the slums of Sao Paulo. I want to read from her diary under the date of December 25. She does not speak of Christmas. She speaks about her son.

"João came in saying he had a stomach-ache," she writes. "I know what it was, for he had eaten a rotten melon. Today they threw a truckload of melons near the river. I don't know why it is that these senseless businessmen come to throw their rotten products near the favela for the children to see and to eat. In my opinion the merchants of Sao Paulo are playing with the people like Caesar when he tortured Christians. But the caesars of today are worse than the Caesars of the past. The others were punished for their faith. And we for our hunger. In that era those who didn't want to die had to stop loving Christ. But we cannot stop loving eating."[1]

The point is that although you don't have an option for life any more, you still don't die. You are killed. And this is an objective difference. If theology is not concerned with this question, even if only as a criticism of religion, all the rest is futile. It might be quite relevant to ask why there is anything at all instead of nothing.

But let us be quick in reasoning this out. More than half of humanity is asking existentially why there is nothing instead of bread on their table.

César Vallejo, a Peruvian poet at the beginning of this century, asked in one of his poems:

> "A man searches for bones and scraps in the dump site.
>   Now shall I write about the infinite?
> A worker falls from the roof, dies, and will no longer
>   eat his lunch.
> Should I then talk about the fourth dimension?"[2]

Common to all of these problems and to the theological endeavor itself is the problem of place. Time and history at the social level is a function of geopolitics. From the struggle of the native inhabitants' rights to their nation's land in Africa or in the Americas to the reality of the slums in the urban areas, from agrarian reform to the conflicts in Central America and the Middle East and Southern Africa, from the demands of black people for a social space to the women's movement, the common quest is for a vital space, a space where the fundamental dimensions of life can flourish in the biological, in the sociological, and in the psychological realms. In this context theology finds itself raising the pertinent issues, finding the signs, widening the road, and following the star that will hopefully guide the way. Theology is called to discern the signs of places!

Displacement is not a metaphor. It is the precise and analytical description of the human condition theology must address in reference to faith. And in addressing it and being challenged by it, theology shares the faith of such people lifting up ensigns over them, as the third Isaiah said (Isaiah 62:3). Such ensigns will point the way to belonging—a way that will lead to a vital space.

This is what distinguishes theology from both science and the church. By not having a territory of its own, by sharing the faith of the displaced in the search for a vital space, theology has a very practical awareness of the sociological relativity of time and space. If time is not a function of a process in which space is created, it is irrelevant.

I recall one of Hegel's axioms that the truth of space is time. I suggest that he was wrong. At least sociologically speaking, the truth of time is space.

At this point I am not challenging either church, or science, or theology. I am only stressing what I regard as a fundamental commitment of theology—a commitment to the search for belonging, of being related to vital space in defense of the life of the poor and dispossessed. Such a commitment is concretely to the people for whom this is in fact a problem, for whom this is a quest.

Now I would like to point to three basic relations of belonging that pertain to theology.

First, there is the relation to God as the ultimate ground of life. This is the proper focus of theology. And it accounts for theology's own displacement. For although this ultimate ground is ubiquitous, its manifestations are always surprising.

Second is the relation to other human beings. Here I'll try to frame the challenge to church and science.

And, third, there is the relation to nature that will raise the challenge that is posed to technology.

♦ RELATION TO GOD AS THE GROUND OF LIFE ♦

The specific function of theology is to reflect on preparing the way to a vital space, which is linked to the religious experience of wonder and awe. Let me call this the doxological function of theology. That doxology is the proper focus of theology is illustrated by the following story.

A camp of peasants who had lost their land and were struggling for agrarian reform was set at the crossing of two major highways in southwest Brazil. More than a thousand women, men, and children were pressing the government to speed up the process of settlement.

A series of problems—with food, with water, with the police—developed during the fifty-four days they were there.

Before the camp was set up, the highway patrol registered an average of one serious accident in every five days at that particular crossing. But in the fifty-four days that the camp lasted, only one such accident occurred: A car ran off the highway at midnight into the middle of the camp, crushing several tents where people were sleeping. For some reason no one was injured.

When a provisional settlement was arranged, the first initiative of the people was to get together for a worship service to thank God, to praise God with their words and songs. They said, "God has been with us. He put his tent right in the middle of where we were."

Anyone looking from outside would regard all those events as nothing more than a mixture of some reasonable organization, and perhaps some luck. Not so for them. They perceived it as the presence of the divine. That moment of worship went beyond a cold analysis of the situation in which they were living—an analysis that they could also do very well. For them it was the eternal breaking in, maybe a *kairos*. In that moment they transcended displacement.

We have records of other such moments. The Bible is full of them: miracles, wonders, epiphanies, signs, and visions that intentionally go beyond analytical precision in language.

Not long ago a tribe of native South Americans were, for the first time, contacted by whites and were presented with a Bible. They had never seen a book. So they didn't have a name for it. When the missionary in the group explained with some effort what that thing was, they finally found a name. They called it "The Skin of God." I think this is a proper way to refer to the images and symbols that remain as records of doxological events. In the reverse sense of the story of the fall in Genesis we can also say that we dress God with some garments of skin, which are also ambiguous.

In situations of displacement, in the craving search for belonging to a vital space, this sense of awe and wonder brings about a wholeness that is quite unexpected. It makes it possible to sing a song, even an impossible song. (An example is the text of Isaiah 42:2 as it responds to the affirmation of Psalm 137, which tells of the impossibility of singing a song to Yahweh in a strange land.) The "no-place" becomes in fact a concrete utopia. It opens up vistas.

This no-place can only be a matter of reflection if we participate in the reality to which it refers, even if we participate only through the skins of God that cover transcendence, but precisely to make it also visible.

The question now is how these moments that I point to as important for the starting of theological reflection determine our common experience of reality. The word "determine," however, is not the appropriate term. Let me use a concept that has some history in Freudian psychology: "overdetermination." We might say that these doxological junctures overdetermine reality. I don't mean to use the concept, however, in the established psychological sense. I want to use it as a category that accounts for the religious sense of being determined by what is over and beyond the description and prescription of our vital conditions and perspectives. It is over and beyond the variables that we control—sociological, biological, physical, and psychological.

The point is that at certain junctures in time and space images, myths, symbols, and rituals have a kairotic impact that evokes doxological moments. We cannot predict them, but they come about. And what difference do they make? We can only reflect about them when they are over, *ex post factum*. In this sense theology is a second act. These moments motivate, prepare, and give us references to face reality in light of God's presence.

Some recent studies in neurobiology have developed the concept of "preparedness."[3] Preparedness is our brain's capability of imagining a preview of things, which is often connected with the religious experience of wholeness. But more than this, it fosters a relation of belonging to the very ground of life itself that we call God. It is not simply a mystic vision of the not-yet, but a sense of being placed in the midst of displacement. This sense animates, motivates, and gives energy.

To reflect about this experience is the old and evasive task of theology, that is, the reading of the meaning of the lines and wrinkles on the skins of God that we have in Scripture and tradition. But above all this is our call to participate in doxological practice, celebrating God's presence where the sense of awe and wonder is indeed present.

The description belonging to the ground of life itself defines even the boundaries of our prose. Paradoxes emerge that push one to appeal to poetry to express it better. Let me illustrate with two lines of poetry that come to mind. The first is from a poem by Holderin called "Patmos." It says something like this: "Close but hard to grasp is the god, but where lies danger grows also what is liberating."[4] Or in the words of Mario Quintana from Brazil, "Please, leave the Other World in peace. Mystery lies here."[5]

♦ CHALLENGE TO THE CHURCH AND SCIENCE ♦

We move now to the second relation of belonging by asking what does "here" mean if mystery lies here?

I have already suggested that the problem we start with is the lack of vital space, in the face of which time disappears. Displacement is distance from vital space. Time is relative to this distance.

Let me illustrate this distance with a tragic example that happened in Brazil recently. In Goiânia, the capital of the state of Goiás, a lead container filled with isotope crystals of Cesium 137 was stolen from a cancer treatment center and sold to a junk dealer. He opened the container with a hammer to remove what he thought would be valuable metal. He then gave the crystals and powder that he found to friends and neighbors as souvenirs. As a result, several blocks were indiscriminately contaminated by radioactivity, with more than one hundred people seriously exposed to radiation. Within forty-five days, four died, turning this into the worst nuclear accident in the world after Chernobyl. The nuclear age entered the homes of families, causing irreversible damage—not because of lack of security in a power plant or because of a bomb, but because of a medical instrument used for cancer treatment that was naively violated.

I use this example because it illustrates a fundamental dilemma posed by the immense distance between the majority of people— particularly but not exclusively those in the dependent world—and science. And I mean science, not technology.

Other examples could be used. Like the absurdity in the application of agrotoxics. Like the lack of control over the pharmaceutical industry. Like drugs that are prohibited in Europe and the United States but are openly sold in the Third World.[6]

What is inaccessible to the people, and this is what makes the difference and establishes the distance, is the knowledge that controls, explains, and fosters technological advances. The very advances of technology increase the democratic responsibility of science. The further we go, the higher we fly, and the greater the difference we establish between levels of understanding of what is going on in our universe, the more responsible we are for the distance we create. The question is not whether we should foster a dialogue between science and the church or the people. It is how and where this is going to happen. We must assume that this is a necessity.

To start answering the question, let me begin with another story. In *The Shepherd of Hermes,* a book of early Christianity, an interesting view of the Christian church is presented. An old woman appears to the main character and gives him a small book. This character tries to guess who this woman is. Since he cannot, another character appears to him and says, "She is the church."

Surprised, the main character asks, "But why is she so old?" It was a good question since the church had just emerged at that time.

The reply from the other character is revealing: "Because she was created first, before all else. That is why she is aged. It was for her that the world was made."[7]

There are fascinating images in this story. We miss the point entirely if we think of church as being simply an institution. The church must be here understood as a community of people, linked and tied by the praxis of love. The statement that the old woman was created first and all the rest was made as a function of her should not be taken in a chronological sense, as in Genesis 1 for example. But maybe we can understand it in the sense of the J account of Genesis 2, where humanity, Adam, appears as a communal being, as the creature of earth that is at the same time a collectivity in an individuality. Adam is a communal being. Without differences yet, Adam is the image of the human made of humus, not yet male or female. That is going to happen later in the account. Not yet shepherd or farmer. There wasn't even a garden. Not yet rich or poor.

This image is transferred to our history to bring up a picture of the church as a community in which life and the means of life are shared, as in Acts 2 and 4. What strikes me in this notion is that humankind, linked in love, is humanity in its lowest, and simultaneously and paradoxically, also in its highest manifestation. We can recall here Psalm 8. Biblical literature in general is characterized by this very tension.

Let us remember the work of Erich Auerbach, *Mimesis,* in which the author finds as being peculiar to the literature of the Old and the New Testament the fusion of the two extremes: that what is lowest, closest to earth, is also what is more like to God.[8]

The true profile of the human (and I want to use the term profile here just to avoid the labyrinth of interpretations of the concept of *imago dei*) is humankind in its minimal condition. These are people living in displacement, that is, without yet having a garden, the poor, the dispossessed, those whom God shapes with special care—but shapes in form of a community. Because these people are left without objective references to recognize their individuality, without having a demarked ground and terrain of their own, they can only be recognized and recognize themselves in intersubjective activity, in being in intimate relationship to each other. Love is the power that fosters this unity. It is the urge toward the unity of what was separated, as Tillich says. This unity fosters a relation of belonging, the second relation of belonging: communal belonging.

Here comes now the challenge to the churches, in the first place, and then to science as well.

The challenge is simply to pass the books of knowledge around. They don't even need to be big books. Small books will suffice, provided they enable the people to prepare their own road to vital space. New vistas then will open, not by focusing on power, in structures, corporations, governments, and legislations, but by being there where the new and primordial profile of the human is being drawn— in communities.

And then we need a science so capable, so sophisticated, as to be simple and democratic. We don't expect science to answer the ethical questions that technology presents to us. We want science to allow us to know the options we have and the implications thereof.

I would like to remind scientists that if the triad—truth, beauty, and simplicity—is in some sense the goal, the more you think you have achieved it (and I am not suggesting that you haven't) the less the people know about it. There is a remarkable difference between cultural and social stages of development achieved particularly in the dependent world in the last one hundred years and the immense speed with which science is progressing. And this gap is always increasing.

If the concepts that I have mentioned—truth, beauty, and simplicity—are somehow universal goals, then scientists are either plainly wrong when they think they have achieved them, or there is a fundamental gap in communication. (I personally think the latter is the case.) An interdisciplinary commitment should be fostered, including pedagogy, cultural anthropology, sociology, psychology, political science, and so forth. Although this post-neopositivist era has taken giant steps in this direction, the challenge remains with us: to move more easily among so many compartmentalized disciplines.

In a similar sense we need churches in which the perplexity of the day of Pentecost might be more repeated and experienced. I paraphrase Acts 2:7-8: "Are not all these who are speaking physicists, biologists, theologians, cosmologists, sociologists? And how is it that we understand them?"

Concretely I am suggesting that the churches may first provide for an ecumenical dialogue that will gather not only different scientists and theologians, but also different religions and non-religious world views, paying close attention to the context from which they emerge. The doctrine of the two natures of Christ formulated as the *communicatio idiomatum,* the transmission of properties between the divine and human natures of Christ, has certainly the central meaning of communicating the divine with the natural. The understanding of this *communicatio* is a task theologians and Christian scientists alike are called to undertake. But *communicatio idiomatum* has also the extended etymological meaning of communicating through different languages. For each language indeed expresses perceptions of reality, whether natural or divine.

This extended sense of *communicatio* brings also a sacramental task that makes the Logos of Christ also dialogical. The Roman Catholic insistence on the church as the *sacramentum mundi,* sacrament of the world, can be understood in this way: a space for *communicatio.* Unfortunately, what we have is still too many instructions and statements and not enough dialogue. An example is the two "instructions" issued by the Vatican Congregation for the doctrine of faith on liberation theology. The first one was a very sharp accusation against liberation theology. Then, through the pressure of Brazilian bishops, there was finally a meeting to discuss liberation theology. And a quite different second "instruction" came after that dialogue.

This dialogue, this *communicatio,* is what makes the difference between the church being *sacramentum mundi* or what Luther once called *magna peccatrix,* the church as the great sinner. To this sacramental task belongs, particularly, the challenge that the church make science available to the people as an operational language— available for the articulation of people's thoughts and dreams so that their needs can flourish in effective actions. This would allow the people to become, I would say, a messianic people, a people aware that they are also those for whom they have been awaiting.

Conversely the church must raise sensitivity and expose science and scientists to the communal life in its search for belonging. I don't mean the popularization of science. I think there is a difference between popularizing something and making it accessible. In want of a better analogy I would say that the people don't need a popular summary of a telephone directory. They need the capacity to use telephone directories.

I am not suggesting we cut the wings of the eagles of science. I am just saying that wherever scientists go and however far they travel, they should be aware that down there, where the creatures of earth live, time is very relative to the space they have. If you do go out in search of a solution to a problem that concerns this generation, it is important to remember that the illustration taken from relativity theory might serve as an analogy on the social level as well. If you travel at the speed of light to the star that will give you the answer you seek in your quest to solve the problems of this generation, you might come back still very young but your generation will be long gone.

♦ CHALLENGE TO TECHNOLOGY ♦

There is another challenge that I am compelled to make. It is directed to technology, and by extension, to science and to the church as well. It comes from the third fundamental relation of belonging. It refers to our relation to nature, including human nature.

I shall use language and concepts that can be understood as very anthropocentric, as an uncritical humanism. The arguments against anthropocentrism have been used to denounce Western Christian disregard for ecological values concerning the human interdependence with the rest of nature. But this argument occasionally slips into an epistomological assertion that knowledge of nature can occur apart from human subjectivity, from human purpose and interest. Although frequently confused with each other, the argument that humankind stands within and not outside nature and the argument that human knowledge can be value-free not only differ but actually contradict each other. My contention is that our discourse about the world in which we live is fundamentally determined by our involvement with it. The truth of such a discourse will depend on the recognition of our organic interaction with this world.

Let me show what I mean by this organic interaction through a biological illustration. All the amazing vitalities in the unfoldings of nature from which life emerges and produces itself are the result of active processes of living organisms. This biological "mechanism" produces the variety, the inner development, and the reproduction of life conditioned by the chemical elements available and informed by the genetic code called DNA. The term "metabolism" is an encompassing notion that applies to the living processes that result in organisms. The same is true of inner human nature.

Now let us take this notion of metabolism as the occasion to make an analogical move, borrowing an insight from Marx's anthropology. There labor plays a central role. Labor is the process in which the human being and nature participate. In it humans, through their actions, mediate, regulate, and control their metabolism with nature under the limiting conditions that nature, including human nature, offers.[9]

The term metabolism is helpful in defining labor in the sense that through labor, human life creates the conditions for the production and reproduction of itself. And, more than this, it creates an intimate involvement of the human with the environment.

Labor is then the human social way of satisfying a need with a determined result (product) informed by an idea. The idea is an image we have of what should come about. It is conditioned by the elements provided in the surrounding environment and by the technical means available to us.

We can call this an external or an economic metabolism as opposed to the inner metabolism of living organisms. But the analogy, I think, works. For this external metabolism not to go wrong and end in an evolutionary dead end, there must be a *homeostasis,* an equilibrium in the exchange that takes place.

Ecological implications follow from this assumption. But the point here is to focus on labor as the point of contact or juncture in relating, distinguishing, and understanding the exchange that happens between the human and nature in order to address the question of anthropocentrism. The question then is, am I being homocentric or anthropocentric by raising labor as the criteria for our relation to the world?

In cosmology since the Big Bang hypothesis, science has been puzzled by what is called the "large number coincidences" in the expansion rates of the universe within the very minimal fractions of the first second. The point is that the expansion rate is precisely that which has allowed for the emergence of life until, further along the evolutionary scale of complexity, human beings appeared. A rate minimally lower or higher would make life as we know it impossible.

From this remarkable coincidence comes what is called the "anthropic principle," which says that what we can expect to observe must be restricted to the conditions necessary for our presence as observers. I don't want, nor am I equipped, to discuss the possible consequences of this principle, like the hypothesis of an ensemble of words not given to our perception or to discuss whether we can resurrect the argument from design.[10] I just appeal to it to make a minimal point suggesting that our discourse about the universe and its unfoldings is precisely and only the observation of our total involvement with it. We are not mere chance outcomes of an evolution. We are involved in each stage of this process from the physical, chemical, and biological up to the sociological and cultural levels as well. And we continue to be involved precisely through the metabolism of labor. This involvement now tells us that we can only speak about a world in which we interact and have been involved.

Thus, because of our involvement, we can say something about it. And nothing that we say is irrelevant to our own existence. It will foster destruction or belonging. Hence we cannot avoid being anthropic. This does not mean being anthropocentric, however, since being anthropic establishes only an epistomological primacy, not an ontological one.

The possibility is there that we have been brought up to be the observers of the privileged place of cockroaches in the evolution, though I believe that we are here to give glory to the God of all creation. In any case, the world that we metabolically recreate is the world that has brought us to be observers of it. We are participant observers and we observe because of our participation.

There is no ecological neutrality. But there are options and these options concern technology as the sophistication of means and tools for the intervention in nature, the extension of our arms. It is not a question of being romantic or not, but of having either a metabolic criterion or of deciding technological questions on the basis of productivity and profit. There is a clear dividing line between these two.

The selective accumulation of the results of labor is to technology what sin is to theology. This is so because when technology becomes a tool of profit it destroys metabolism. It takes the environment out of the control of those who intervene directly in it and are affected by the consequences. Simultaneously it controls the use of the means or tools for intervention in this very reality. The result is the destruction of metabolism. The option therefore is to be metabolic (bringing together) instead of being diabolic (throwing apart).

An interesting illustration of this "diabolism" and its consequences is Pizzaro's conquering of the Inca empire in what is now
modern Peru. What happened was not a simple plunder of the Inca
gold. It was the destruction of a highly functional and fairly equali-
tarian society homeostatically adjusted to the environment—and the
mountains of Peru are a very harsh environment. This adjustment
did not occur through a naive and romantic submission to nature
but through high technological development, particularly in the fields
of engineering, agriculture, politics, and astronomy. These achievements were comparable, and sometimes superior, to the standards
achieved in Europe at the same time and in the same fields. The
difference was that Europe, and Spain in particular, had the technology of war and navigation.

My claim is that the metabolism of labor provides the foundation
for a scientific de-anthropomorphizing of reality. It is therefore labor
that is not only a condition for the knowledge of nature itself, but
simultaneously also the ground for an ethics of knowledge. The only
authentic scientific endeavor must be in the last analysis committed
to this metabolism. It is on this basis that knowledge itself is ultimately
grounded and nature, human and non-human nature alike, is itself
respected.

Much is at stake. Many more specific challenges hound us than
those that I have lifted here. The possibility of a nuclear holocaust
is at the distance of a mad finger. Famine kills and sub-nutrition is
undoing evolution, creating generations of sub-*homo sapiens*. We
cannot afford floating in the galactic space of clean dogmatics, aseptic
science, comfortable liturgics, caring pews, and merely efficient technology. We have got to get in touch with the stuff we are made from
and smell it and taste it until we fall in love with it again. Then we
may be spared from ourselves and find joy in an organic science, an
organic theology, an organic church, an organic technology. The risk
is to keep navigating for its own sake.

I finish with an old *fado*. A *fado* is a Portuguese folk song. This
one goes back to the decadence of the Portuguese empire when
Portugal could maintain itself only through the plunder gathered in
its sailing missions. The song says, "To sail is necessary. To live is no
longer a need."

Let us not sing this song.

NOTES

1. Carolina Maria de Jesus, *Child of the Dark* (New York: Signet, 1962), pp.
   124–125.
2. César Vallejo, *Obras Completas VIII: Poemas Humanos* (Barcelona: Laia,
   1977), p. 87.
   "Un hombre . . . busca en el fango huesos, cascaras

¿Como escribir, despues, del infinito?
Un albanil cae de un techo, muere y ya no almuerza . . .
¿Hablar, despues, de cuarta dimension?"

3. See, for example, Edith Turner, "Encounter with Neurobiology: The Response of Ritual Studies" in *Zygon* 21/2 (1986), pp. 219–32, and other articles in the same issue of the journal.

4. Friedrich Hölderlin, *Gedichte-Hyperion* (Munchen: Wilhelm Goldmann, 1978), p. 138.
"Nah ist
Und schwer zu fassen der Gott,
Wo aber Gefahr ist, wächst
Das Rettende auch."

5. Mario Quintana, *Diário Poético* (Porto Alegre: Globo, 1985), 24/02.

6. Gary Gereffi, *The Pharmaceutical Industry and Dependency in the Third World* (Princeton: Princeton University Press, 1983).

7. *Apud* Juan Luis Segundo, *The Community Called Church,* translated by John Drury (Maryknoll, N.Y.: Orbis, 1973), p. 7.

8. Erick Auerbach, *Mimesis: Dargestellte Wirklichkeit in der abendländischen Literatur* (Bern: A. Francke, 1946).

9. See Karl Marx, *Das Kapital,* 3 vols. (Berlin: Dietz, 1947), 1:192. See also 1:57; 3:723, 728, *passim.*

10. John Leslie, "Anthropic Principle, World Ensemble, Design," *American Philosophical Quarterly* 19/2 (1982), pp. 141–51.

◆4◆

The Challenge of the Church to Science and Theology

Gerhard Liedke

In the first part of my paper I shall reflect on the form the church takes in relation to the challenges of our time. In the second part I shall deal with the claims on science that come out of such a vision of the church. In the third part I shall comment on the church's claims on theology.

◆ PEACE, JUSTICE, AND THE KEEPING OF CREATION ◆

No church dare be an end within itself. Every form the church takes must ask itself the question: How can the kingdom of God and his *shalom* be expressed? The kingdom of God, to be sure, does not have its origin in this world. Yet it acquires its form in this creation. So if the present challenges of this world are properly expressed in the World Council of Churches' formula for the conciliar process, "Peace, Justice, and Integrity of Creation," then the question concerning *shalom* can be stated more precisely as pertaining to the church's contribution to peace, justice, and the keeping of creation.

Inherent in expressing this *shalom* is the reduction of violence. Only by reducing the violence of humanity over nonhuman creation can we make a contribution to the keeping of creation. Only through abating the violence the rich carry out against the poor can we accomplish our contribution to justice. Only by lessening the violence among nations and within nations can we accomplish our contribution to the reality of peace. The central question asked of the shape of a church before the Second Coming of Christ is: How does that church conduct itself in regard to social, political, and scientific-technical power and violence? Yet the customary definitions of the church remain strangely silent in the face of this question.

A look into the history of churches shows that at various times and in various places they have taken four different shapes:

1. the early Christian peace model
2. the liturgical-eucharistic model
3. the super-church model
4. the liberation-church model

The *early Christian peace model* is based on the fact that in Jesus a new possibility for human, social, and political relationships appears. In this model the church as a small group lives out a nonviolent example in opposition to the violent structures of the large societies. The church groups do not actively politic in the direction of changing structures. They threaten the structures, instead, by existing in a different way.

The Mennonites, Quakers, and Brethren—communities that have formed themselves as a reaction to the present crises in many countries—play an important and fruitful role. These small communities try to work responsibly ecologically. They live in a fellowship of common wealth and experiment with new economic structures. They intensively engage in nonviolent methods against oppression. Refusing to bear arms has been a main characteristic of such communities since their beginning.

In the *liturgical-eucharistic model* the otherness of Jesus' disciples is proclaimed in a different way. This model emphasizes participation in the body of Christ through the worship experience and through the fellowship of love to one another. It is most clearly developed in the Orthodox churches of the East. Worship and meditation about God, who in himself is the fellowship of love, and the eucharistic celebration are the starting points when these churches want to express their responsibility for justice, peace, and the integrity of creation.

The *super-church model* often develops where the small alternative church groups are also successful. It adjusts within the limits set by societal and state power and authority. It tries to establish criteria for partaking in power and to define the limits of participation. In this way the super-church teaching concerning the righteous war and the law of the Middle Ages against usury is to be understood.

Even the super-church model knows about prophetic opposition and the prophetic message to the powers that be. Prophetic meddling has, as in the Bible, two purposes in relation to the institutions of power: nonacceptance and/or constructive transformation of the existing structures.

The *liberation church model,* similar to the super-church, seeks to involve Christians in the formation of power and the influence of the church on the use of power. The difference is that it is strongly oriented toward the priority of the poor. Priority is given to empowering the powerless. In extreme cases the use of opposing violence is not excluded, as long as this opposing violence breaks or lessens oppressive violence. The liberation church, however, is not interested only in the taming of power. It is interested in its transformation.

These four models, found in the history of the church, are obviously "ideal cases" that never realize themselves in a pure form. In most cases elements of various models are mixed in an empirical church.

The weaknesses of each model need also to be noted. The peace church model is in danger of letting itself be forced into a ghetto in which it struggles to survive instead of witnessing provocatively. The liturgical-eucharistic model can be used to elevate and glorify the worldly powers that be. In church history this is known as "byzantinism."

The super-church model is especially prone to the temptation of denying its prophetic elements and of accommodating itself totally to the power and authority in an existing society. Only participation in power remains, as is illustrated in large measure in the formation of the Reformation churches in Europe. This silencing of prophetic criticism is frequently based on the modern belief in the integrity of the internal laws of each particular area of life (for instance, the area of business). Then the church has nothing to add except a certain sharpening of the conscience.

For the liberation church model it is valid to say that even the controlled act of opposing violence must be disputed, for the church cannot point to the example of Jesus. When the liberation church is successful, it experiences problems similar to those of the super-church.

Listing these points of criticism reveals the following insights: The actual danger in the shape the church takes is its adaptation to worldly power and violence. Existing church bodies are in great danger of this even if their starting point is the liturgical-eucharistic or the liberation church. Less endangered are the peace church initiatives. With them, however, lurks the danger of self-satisfaction and the loss of the "salt power" of the gospel.

In the meantime it is important to see what the church can learn from all four models. From the liturgical-eucharistic model it can learn that the renewal-of-the-world form of the church always comes through the eucharist and in the meditation of godly life. That is why the spirituality of the Orthodox churches is so important.

From the super-church model the church can learn that, from a certain point on, participation in worldly power cannot be avoided. Then all depends on how it carries through on its spiritual and peace and liberation-church moments in the new situation.

From the liberation church model it can learn the biblical option for the poor. This option will not only be expressed in the form of caritative sympathy but in the form of societal transformation, so that the poor really gain social power.

Finally it can learn from the peace church model that every participation in power entangles it in unavoidable guilt. Therefore the nonviolent strategies and the formation of small alternative communities are always and ever again unavoidable.

Summarized once again: In view of the challenge of our times it is necessary from biblical and historical experience to demand of the churches (1) that they carry out nonacceptance of unrighteousness and violence and that they provide prophetic criticism; (2) that they encourage alternative communities and thereby spread love of the enemy and encouragement for the poor; and (3) that they engage in constructive love in the taming and transformation of power structures, starting with the giving of power to the powerless.

What now results for science and theology, the two other points of the triangle, from a church described like this?

◆ CLAIMS OF THE CHURCH ON SCIENCE ◆

Churches that have clarified their own relationship to power and violence will make the question of power and violence the main question directed to science.

Making this question plausible for science, however, is not easy. Many scientists still dispute that the work of present-day scientists, technicians, and engineers is involved in violence against nature and against humanity. Scientists, and also business people, wince at this point. Such an evaluation of their work and our Western life-style is altogether too unfamiliar. Scientists understand their scientific and technical work and the world resting on it as being morally neutral and therefore incapable of violence. The results of science first become ethical for them in the hands of the so-called employers. In most cases politicians are named.

This tenacious view of the neutrality of technology, science, and business must be rejected. This has already happened to an extent through such researchers as Werner Heisenberg, Carl Friedrich von Weizsaecker, Guenter Howe, and Georg Picht. They have pointed out that the founding fathers of modern science and technology (for example, Rene Descartes and Francis Bacon) were quite clear as to the character of power and violence in modern science and technology. Power means the ability to do what I want to do. Violence is a manifestation of power.

Francis Bacon differentiates among three levels of human aspiration to power and violence. The lowest level is "to make valid one's own power in one's own country" (thus national politics). On the second level "the estimation and the power of the native land among other nations is to be furthered" (thus international politics). The third level is the highest and most respectable aspiration to power. It is "the power and dominion of humankind over the whole of nature."

On the first level, in terms of national affairs, we have found relatively nonviolent forms of resolving conflicts. On the second level, on the international scene, we have not achieved nearly as much. On the third level violence is carried out now as before in the dominion over the natural world. That is why we talk about the "victory procession of technology." That is why in science it is always a case of subjugating nature. In the current ecological crisis we have won the war for humanity against nature. Nature experiences our force with suffering and destruction. Such ecological systems as the rain forests are threatened by collapse.

At the beginning of this path stood the determination for power over nature. Science is power, as Bacon himself said.

The scientific-technological violence against nature is measurable, technically measurable. Our energy budget is a good indication of our violent rule over nature. The more humanity uses energy, the more violence is carried out against non-human creation. *Nota bene:* Not every use of energy is violent, but the use of energy sets the measure for our scientific-technical violence against nature.

The church implores science and scientists to evaluate their allegedly morally neutral work. Such evaluations could become the foundation for new behavior. This new behavior would be evident as every future scientific act would contribute to the reduction of violence against nature and to the minimization of violence in human affairs.

One could call this—in terms of a slogan—a mitigating science and technology. The first goal of a mitigating science must be the reduction of specific energy usage per product. Studies in the Federal Republic of Germany have shown that many products and services could be produced in like quality with fifty percent of the energy. I refer, for example, to new methods in the production of aluminum and to new insulation techniques, which can significantly reduce the energy usage for the heating of a home. I also think of the fact that the future of agriculture will not be found in an energy-intensive green revolution, but in energy-saving, close-to-nature methods of cultivation.

Working out the details for such a mitigating technology is not the task of the church. The church's task is loudly and clearly to demand of science that there be a reduction in the violence that has evolved from it up until now. If the new areas of microelectronics and genetic technology are called into view, then the result will be that in full realization of the grave problems we have in these new areas important new impulses to save energy will come from both.

The promotion of a mitigating science and technology is in no way an enemy of technology, nor is it oriented toward the Stone Age. Rather it allows such mitigation to be brought into relationship with advanced technological research—only, however, measured by the proper goal of continuing to reduce growing violence.

Overcoming the view of the neutrality of science and gaining the goal of a nonviolent science and technology is naturally connected to more than the use of energy. The symbol of science today for lay people is a diagram with a continuously rising curve. This symbol indicates the close connection between science and business. As long as growth is valued as the foundational principle of the economy, without which there can be no healthy economy, the limits will not be seen. It may be methodically correct that research cannot recognize any taboos and must always strike forth into new territory. What is methodically proper and successful, however, must not without examination be made into the foundational principle of business and politics. We have known since the Club of Rome studies that a limitless growth on a limited planet is in principle not possible.

For this reason research projects and scientific and technical projects do not continually have to surpass their previous projects in size. Is it reasonable to construct bombs that are more powerful? Is it reasonable to send spaceships beyond the moon? Is it reasonable to extend the life of old people through technical advances when on the other side of the globe millions of children are dying?

In all of these instances the church must demand that science and technology revise the boundlessness of its work and delineate its boundaries. Perhaps later such boundaries will be extended into new areas. At our time in history, however, it is important that the existence of limits be recognized by science.

Practically, the result will be that science will deal with the research of the smaller things, such as the development of local technologies. The environmental relationship between humankind and nature, which today is being pulverized by gigantic massive projects of technology, must be regarded as the main area of research for science. The saying that evolved years ago is simply true: Humanity must not travel to the moon until the problems of hunger on our planet have been solved.

It follows quite rightly that the church should demand of science that its overly optimistic view of humanity be revised. Science still perceives man as a rational being with its emotions under control and more or less functioning within the laws set by science. Only in light of this view of humanity can we understand the fact that we have allowed such gigantic risk technologies as nuclear energy, space travel, the atomic bomb system, and mass automobile transit. Such systems actually function only under the condition that the people who work within them make no mistakes. As we try to eliminate human mistakes through automation and computer guidance, the systems become forcibly inhumane. Even so the human factor cannot be eliminated. It simply wanders in the programmed mistakes. Less violent science and technology must therefore become amicable toward mistakes. It must construct less massive systems in which mistakes can be forgiven and not result in massive catastrophes. Amicability towards mistakes and small system size belong close together.

The demand also needs to be heard that science and technology can be recallable and reversible in their consequences. Energy production that for generations destroys forests or irreversibly leaves atomic waste for 20,000 years is too much violence for our planet.

In the end the church must stand up to that feature of scientific power that divides and conquers. From this principle of division and separation the gulf between rich and poor occurs again and again. The industrial nations with twenty-six percent of the earth's population own eighty percent of all production. Conversely seventy-four percent of humanity in the poor countries dispose of twenty percent of all resources. This imbalance results from a science and technology that has been violent up to this point. We all know that the gap between the poorest and richest countries widened over and over in the last decades.

In summary of this part of my paper, I state: The church asks science for the development of a new prototype for scientific and technological work. This prototype must understand and realize such values as mitigation, appropriateness, communication, reversibility, and participation. Today science itself is an instrument of oppression and so leads further and further into the crises, against which both science and the church must, in common, defend themselves.

◆ CLAIMS OF THE CHURCH ON THEOLOGY ◆

Churches that have reflected on their relationship to power and violence and have found a new position will make demands also on

Christian theology. While science presents itself in the countries of the West and East, and of the North and South, in somewhat the same way, the case is different with theology. Theology is propagated differently in North America compared to Europe, in South America compared to Asia and Africa. I speak here of theology that can be called "indigenous" and not about the acceptance of Northern and Western theologies in the Southern part of the earth. As a member of a church of the West and of the North I can therefore only formulate the demands that can be directed toward, shall we say, North Atlantic theology.

The direction of the demands to be mentioned here follow generally from the fact that theology (from the Middle Ages up to the present) has understood itself as being a part of science. Certainly not in all its branches and all its areas, but structurally it moves within the realm of the European university as a specialized science beside other sciences. It takes part in the power structure of the sciences, even if in a more subtle manner. It partakes in the deductive process together with other sciences. It participates in the power pretension of theory over against an application that has to conform to the theories.

Theology's claim to power over against church practice cannot be maintained. More and more it is becoming clear that theology is only possible as the reflection of Christian experience and church practice. Theology—including biblical theology—can never be the first step. It must always be the second step, reflecting on church practice and then therapeutically educating. The faith of the church and the faith of the individual Christian properly precedes theological reflection. It is a true form of power and violence when a theology in an exegetical area, for example, orients itself according to the norms of modern critical historical and exegetical science, judges the biblical statements, and then makes rules for the faith of Christians in regard to what can stand as faith and what cannot. In German theology we experienced this in the debate about demythologization. The scientific understanding of reality at that time excluded the resurrection of Jesus Christ as a continuing reality among other realities. It had to be toned down to a simple datum of interpretation. Similarly the charismatic elements of biblical and present faith could not be theologically honored. They connected to phenomena that, oriented on science, were not to be accommodated even in theology.

Naturally theologians of this epoch always gave reassurance that it was not their intent to use power in the way in which they carried out theology. But factually it happened anyway. Thereby theology often did not notice that especially in the toughest science, in physics, the methodical narrow-mindedness of the nineteenth century was overcome in the twentieth century. Wider ranging concepts are now available. Only hesitantly has theology accepted the possibilities of a larger understanding of reality. Therefore the church will have to call upon theology at least to do that which is a possibility in the present understanding of science.

Beyond that, however, it is questionable if theology in principle can subjugate itself even to a wider-ranging understanding of science. It can do this only if science no longer understands itself as primarily the bearer of power over humankind and nature. With this main claim it is not meant that logical thinking and tenacious and exact theological research be invalidated or despised. The criteria of criticism must be developed in the area of theology, of faith, and of the life of the church and may not be taken over from scientific categories.

Theology as a whole has become completely too rational. It needs to understand in a completely new way that the life of the church has a liturgical-eucharistic dimension. The more we in the Western churches learn from the churches of the East, the more our theology can follow through on this learning process. The concentration of Protestant theological education on the sermon can no longer be kept up. The worship service must not be solely planned and prepared by the pastor but by a responsible team from the congregation. The permanent Protestant strain of speaking and hearing needs to be supplemented by such meditative elements as those that take place in the worship services of the Community of the Brothers of Taize. The question of such liturgical gestures as the exchange of the peace needs to become the object of theological research.

Theology also must remove itself from its normal neutrality, copied from science, over and against the life of the church. In the German churches, after the bad experiences of the Hitler regime, a new reflecting began in regard to participation of the churches in state power and force. But it has not been followed through far enough. The churches still are too strongly interwoven into the structure of the state. Theology has cast very little light upon the existing relationships. So we in the churches of the Evangelical Church in Germany, for instance, stand before the problem that a change in the state tax laws would directly affect the income of the church. Here we are purely passive receivers of state measures. No one in our theology has really enlightened us in the last decades about these relationships. So we in the churches now wake up and rub our eyes.

The way in which theology is carried out in a country and in a church naturally depends very strongly upon the method of theological education. That is why the church must set demands in regard to the education of its theologians and pastors. It is very unsatisfactory that our pastors study theology for four or five years and then during their thirty-year careers actually only concern themselves with questions of theology out of private interest, and that means mostly not at all. On the other hand it is just as unsatisfactory that most academic teachers do not serve as the pastor of a congregation for a long period of time.

"I don't want to say anything that will hurt," Dietrich Ritschl stated in this regard, "but in the last instance I trust no theological teacher—besides perhaps an expert in the field of exegesis and history—who has not been a pastor for a long time, visited the old and the infirm, buried children and young people, and every Sunday had to, even if nothing new came into his head, let himself be heard by his congregation."[3]

This state of affairs relates to the fact that so-called practical theology has been separated from biblical-exegetical, from historical, and from systematic theology. That separation conforms to the understanding that in practical theology one only has to "put" the theoretical theology "into" practice. Because of systematic theology's failure to relate to practice, it has for the most part established itself in the heads of theology students only as a historical discipline.

This is not the place to reconsider all the consequences for the fashioning of theology, only a few impulses because of the importance of the theme: The study at the beginning of a pastor's or theologian's career must concentrate on the most important things, then after fifteen years in the calling, a life-long education in theology should take place in the form of yearly courses. Those teaching theology would need to adjust to this new form of education and be brought to the understanding that practice has preference over theory. Without a doubt theology would come to concern itself more with the whole person and with all sectors of society. The business of theology presently suffers under the problem that, where it deals with the problems of life, it deals with problems geared to theologians in their twenties.

I have claimed here that theology should be the second step after the practice of the faith of the church and that theology therefore must acquire a certain modesty vis-a-vis present-day demands for power. It must now also be said that the stepping forth of theology out of its moral neutrality also demands that theological patterns of thought be developed for producing clear judgments regarding requests from Christians and churches in terms of their practice. Theology must not be satisfied with the proclamation of general maxims and principles. It must concretely carry out the principle of the reduction of violence within technical options, for instance in regard to energy consumption. Too often contemporary theology does not want to soil its hands at this point, for the possibility of false judgments is naturally present. On the other hand, theology cannot offer adequate help by just working out only one Christian option for action for a problem. The duty of theology is to research the various results of different options for action and to build up the area of decision-making.

For this work it may be profitable if theology would orient more toward the applied methods of social science: the methods for the testing of hypotheses. For a certain problem area (for instance, the relationship between eschatology and ethics) a so-called zero hypothesis could be set up, investigating the present understanding of the problem in the churches. This hypothesis would then have to be verified, or conversely rejected as false, through the use of biblical material, of the history of the church, of present Christian teaching models, and also of non-Christian suggestions for the solution to the problem. The results could then find their outcome in a second problem—and solution—developed from the first hypothesis. A new research team could again utilize this gained hypothesis as a zero hypothesis for the starting point of a new theological project.

It is evident that such theological work could not be carried out by theological soloists, but only in teamwork by the representatives of the most varied theological and nontheological disciplines. Until now the development of scientific theology has been too dependent on the created problems of scientific imminence by singular theologians. Only seldom is it achievable to organize theology as project work. That must, however, be maintained as a demand of the church on theology.

Now something in closing: Churches that have clarified their relationship to power and authority must urgently ask theology to reflect on the statement regarding the omnipotence of God. The theological statements in the past regarding the omnipotence of God reflect too much the intertwining of empirical churches with the powers-that-be. It should have become clear today that one cannot speak of the omnipotence of God in the sense of an observation about the world and all its facts. The biblical statements in which one speaks of the omnipotence of God are without exception statements of praise and not of theological teaching.

If theology is to follow behind the practical experiences of Christians and churches its starting point must be that God's power finds itself in battle against unrighteousness, hatred, discord, and the destruction of creation. Theology must result from the faithfulness and love of God toward a world that, for the most part, abandons and scorns him. Only in eschatological praise can the omnipotence of God be believed and hoped in. One can speak about the omnipotence of God only at the end of a theological discussion.

NOTES

1. Ulrich Duchrow & Gerhard Liedke, *Schalom—der Schoepfung Befreiung, den Menschen Gerechtigkeit, den Voelkern Frieden* (Stuttgart, 1987).
2. Gerhard Liedke, *Im Bauch des Fisches,* fourth ed. (Stuttgart: Oekologische Theologie, 1984).
3. Dietrich Rischl, *Zur Logik der Theologie* (Muenchen, 1984), p. 347.
4. J. H. Yoder, *Die Politik Jesu—der Weg des Kreuzes* (Maxdorf, 1981).

•5•

The Task of the Church in the New Scientific Age

Harold P. Nebelsick

The task of the church in the new scientific age, as in every age, is to be the church. From the Reformed perspective this means taking *ecclesia reformata semper reformanda,* the church reformed always to be reformed, with utmost seriousness. (The gerundive case of the term *reformanda* is of first importance. It should be translated "to be reformed," not "reforming.") Although in the context of seventeenth-century Protestant orthodoxy this called for the church to be reformed according to the Word of God as heard in Scripture, the Word of God is *ipso facto* always a contemporary word. It addresses the age in which it is spoken. According to Luke, for example, the Apostle Paul explained God to the Greeks by citing the Stoic poet Aratus, "In him we live and move and have our being" (Acts 17:28). So today we might say, "We live and move and have our temporal being under the aegis of science and technology."[1]

Our hermeneutics is supported by the history of the development of science in the West. To follow such diverse people as Gunter Howe, Reijer Hooykass, Stanley Jaki, and Thomas F. Torrance, that development was encouraged by the ability to see and understand reality through the eyeglasses of Scripture. According to this interpretation, the revival of interest in the world of antiquity, which in the eleventh through the fifteenth centuries brought about the Renaissance, resuscitated interest in the biblical documents as well. The renewed emphasis on the biblical doctrines of God, creation, humankind, and redemption eventually led to a reorientation of the European mind regarding nature and the place of humankind in it. This served to prepare the ground for the seeds of science that had come from the ancient world to take root and grow. The seventeenth-century scientific revolution, the basis of "The New Scientific Age" that we are addressing, was the result.[2]

As a consequence science, and with it technology, has come about. Science has taught us to penetrate into the rationality of nature. With technology, by which we manipulate nature, we have literally revolutionized the way we view and utilize reality.

At the same time that we have learned to use nature for our benefit, however, we have also been enabled to endanger and destroy it. Whereas in the pre-scientific era we often stood before nature in fear and trembling, nature now has good reason to fear and tremble before us.

It would seem quite obvious, therefore, that we need a new clarification of the relationship of humankind and nature.

In that we continue to confess that the Word of God comes to us in relation to the biblical documents, a primary task of the church in the new scientific age is to understand nature and our relationship to nature in the light of Scripture. That understanding may well lead to the development of a new correlation between the doctrines of salvation and creation. Were we then to act as we believe, our basic understanding of nature and of our relationship to it would have a bearing on the way we pursue science and technology.

A biblical understanding may encourage us to see the destiny of humankind and the destiny of nature as being inextricably inter-twined and interdependent. That understanding may motivate us to probe nature in an attempt to understand it at its depths. It may also enable us to cooperate with it more adequately than is now possible as well as embolden us to set limits to our interaction. Thus we may be enabled to determine methods and standards for making orderly determinations as to what is to be done, how it is to be done, and what ought to be left undone.

The thesis of what I say here is based on the *Goeltinger Theologen-Physiker Gespraeche* that took place on a yearly basis between 1949 and 1961. With these conversations, the depth of which has yet to be duplicated, the modern ecumenical dialogue between theology and natural science had its beginning.

The task of the church is to proclaim God as the sovereign God, the Lord of Creation that is contingent upon him.   The priestly account of creation in Genesis 1-2:4a presents God as sovereign Lord who begins the beginning by creating the heavens and the earth. He spoke and creation was brought forth as an ordered continuum. The light was called forth and separated from the darkness. The firmament, as it was believed, separated the waters above from the waters below. Water and land were separated from one another. The earth was commanded to bring forth plants bearing seed and trees bearing fruit (v. 11-12). Sun, moon, and stars were placed in the heavens. The waters were filled with living creatures, the air with birds that flew across the firmament. The animals, like the plants, were brought forth from the earth and the animals were classified.

Creation, however, was not yet finished.

To create humankind, God took special counsel (v. 26). "Let us make Adam (humankind)." Rather than being brought forth "naturally" from the ground as were the plants and animals, humankind was made in the "image of God," after God's "likeness." The "special creation" was followed by the command that humankind rule over the other creatures.

The words, "Let them have dominion," would seem to imply that humankind's likeness to God is a reflection of God's authority. As God is the lord over the totality of creation, so humans are appointed God's viceroys, his ministers, as far as the other creatures are concerned. The dominion is made explicit in v. 28: "Be fruitful and multiply, and fill the earth and subdue it; and have dominion over the fish of the sea and over the birds of the air and over every living thing that moves upon the earth."

Humankind is thus given the awesome responsibility before God of subduing the earth and ruling its non-human creatures. This sounds very much like a command to pursue science and technology. Humankind is ordered to take on the terrifying task of taking charge of the world. That task can be fulfilled only if we learn about nature—science—and apply that knowledge to nature— technology.

Historian Lynn White corroborates the judgment that the command has influenced our relationship to nature. His judgment of the matter, however, is negative rather than positive. In his 1967 article, "The Historical Roots of our Ecologic Crisis," White claims that the relationship between humankind and the world, which has resulted in the continuing destruction of nature, has come about because of "the orthodox Christian arrogance toward nature" following "the imperative of the Genesis command."[3]

There is no doubt that the Hebrew word *kibbes,* which is properly translated "subdue," may refer to rather stringent activity. It is used, for instance, in making someone into a slave or taking advantage of another's labor. In its Genesis setting, however, the command to have dominion is an expression of humankind's "likeness" to God. Humankind is to represent God's dominance over creation and express his loving, caring rule over it. Rather than giving the right of exploitation, "dominion" is to be understood as "service." The dominion over the creatures is thus to be compared to that of a shepherd who protects his flock from the wild beasts or a farmer who keeps the cattle out of the fields. Humans are God's gardeners, shepherds, and farmers.

The task of the church is to proclaim that humankind, under God, is responsible for order in God's earthly creation. In contradistinction to Lynn White, who puts the blame for our present "ecologic crisis" on the Genesis command, it is more accurate to see the whole account of Genesis as having an "ecological structure." There is a proper harmony of all the components of creation, in general, and of the ecosystem, in particular. There is a balance between light and darkness. There is a firmament to protect the earth from the "waters above." The sun, moon, and stars have their special places in the heavens and relate to the earth in giving light. The plants, birds, aquatic creatures, and different species of animals all have their particular and appropriate habitats.

Even the food is designated. Whereas the animals are to eat "every green plant," humankind is told to eat those plants that need cultivation and are under agricultural management, the grains and the fruit of the trees.

"Behold, I have given you every plant yielding seed which is upon the face of all the earth, and every tree with seed in its fruit; you shall have them for food" (Gen. 1:29).

God's command to "subdue the earth" is originally the authorization to engage in agriculture in order to produce the needed food supply. Just as God dominates and rules his world with care, so humankind rules the animals and cultivates and preserves the earth.

The task of the church is to proclaim that sin distorts creation. Genesis 1 is "pre-history." It is "pre-fall," and we live "after the fall." In the Yahwist narrative of Genesis 2 and following, the symbiosis with nature is expressed equally strongly, if not more strongly than in Genesis 1. Humankind is constituted of the elements of nature itself.

"Then the Lord God formed man of dust from the ground, and breathed into his nostrils the breath of life; and man became a living being" (Gen. 2:7).

God formed the creatures as well "out of the dust of the ground." He paraded the animals before Adam "to see what he would call them." Adam's naming of the creatures expresses his dominion over them.

When humans, dissatisfied with their subservient role, want to be like God and rebel against God, the whole of nature is affected. Adam and Eve's sin not only causes them to be driven from the garden, it causes the harmonious relationship between God and humankind, human and human, and humankind and nature to be disturbed. Estrangement, pain, and suffering result.

The serpent is cursed to go upon its belly and eat dust and be the enemy of humankind. The woman is cursed to endure pain in childbearing and to be subservient to her husband. The ground is cursed to bring forth thorns and thistles. Adam is cursed to toil in the field until he "returns to the ground" from which he was taken (Gen. 3:14ff).

Jealousy arises between brother and brother. Cain murders Abel, and again the ground is affected. "When you till the ground, it shall no longer yield to you its strength" (Gen. 4:12a). Cain is banished from the presence of the Lord to wander on the earth (Gen. 4:12ff). As the narrative continues, wickedness increases. Human hearts are filled with evil (Gen. 6:5).

"Now the earth was corrupt in God's sight and the earth was filled with violence. And God saw the earth and behold, it was corrupt, for all flesh had corrupted their way upon the earth" (Gen. 6:11-12).

The task of the church is to proclaim that God makes his covenant with humankind and that covenant includes all of nature. God repented of his creation and decided to blot it out with the flood. But not even the flood was to destroy either humankind or the animals of God's creation. The ark provided the lifeboat. And after the lifeboat landed, there was a new start for Noah, his descendants, and all God's creatures that had been taken along for the ride to the new beginning.

Significantly, the blessing of Genesis 1:28 is repeated in 9:1-4. There are, however, notable alterations. "Be fruitful and multiply and fill the earth. The fear of you and the dread of you shall be upon every beast of the earth and upon every bird of the air, upon everything that creeps on the ground, and all the fish of the sea; into your hand they are delivered. Every moving thing that lives shall be food for you; and as I gave you the green plants I give you everything. Only you shall not eat flesh with its life, that is, its blood."

Noah is to respect nature even as he utilizes it for food. All the creatures are delivered into human hands. Again the green plants are given for food and the animals are added to the menu. Nonetheless, this does not give permission for exploitation. Animals, like humans, have a *nephesh,* a soul. The eating of the animals is not to include the eating of their blood with which the *nephesh* was thought to be bound.

The earth is God's earth. The animals are God's animals. God will require a reckoning of every beast as well as of every person (Gen. 9:5). God makes his covenant with Noah and his descendants but he makes it also with "every living creature," "the birds," "the cattle," and "every beast of the earth" (Gen. 9:10f). The covenant made with Noah has to do with humankind, the animals, and the earth.

"I establish my covenant with you, that never again shall all flesh be cut off by the waters of a flood, and never again shall there be a flood to destroy the earth" (Gen. 9:11).

It is from the earth that Noah is allowed to live. Noah becomes "a tiller of the soil" and he plants a vineyard (Gen. 9:20). To till the soil, which in Hebrew is *abad,* is to "serve the earth." It may be significant that the term is also used in relationship to the worship of God.

The Genesis attitude toward the land and its creatures indicates the Old Testament attitude toward nature as a whole. The ground belongs to God. In Leviticus 25:4 the ground is of such import that it is part of the Sabbath command.

"But in the seventh year there shall be a sabbath of solemn rest for the land, a sabbath to the Lord; you shall not sow your field or prune your vineyard."

According to Leviticus 26:3ff, God promises abundant harvests and peace in the land as a reward for obedience. Disobedience, however, is to be punished by a rebellion of nature.

"You shall therefore keep all my statutes and all my ordinances, and do them; that the land where I am bringing you to dwell may not vomit you out" (Lev. 20:22).

Obverse to the way we value people over the environment, Leviticus goes so far as to be at least as much concerned for the land as for the people.

"Then the land shall enjoy its sabbaths as long as it lies desolate, while you are in your enemies' land; then the land shall rest, and enjoy its sabbaths. As long as it lies desolate it shall have rest, the rest which it had not in your sabbaths when you dwelt upon it" (Lev. 26:34f, cf. v. 43).

The Deuteronomist continues to emphasize this respect for animals and land. A bird with its eggs may not be disturbed (Deut. 22:6). An ox is not to be muzzled on the threshing floor (Deut. 25:4).

To summarize, God commanded Adam and Eve to be in charge of creation and to live with it in harmony. They are to keep the land and rule the creatures. In reciprocation, the land will keep humankind. The sin of Adam and Eve, however, has a direct effect on lowering the yield of the earth's abundance, and the ground refuses to cooperate with Cain, the sinner. God's blessing and curse are intricately intertwined with the relationship between the way humankind acts and the way the earth responds. God makes a covenant with Noah as well as with the non-human creatures. He promises never to destroy the earth by flood again.

The task of the church is to proclaim that God will redeem creation. Eventually, as Isaiah looks forward to the reestablishment of God's rule, there is to be full reconciliation of the whole of creation:

The wolf shall dwell with the lamb,
>   and the leopard shall lie down with the kid,
and the calf and the lion and the fatling together,
>   and a little child shall lead them.
The cow and the bear shall feed;
>   their young shall lie down together;
>   and the lion shall eat straw like the ox.
The sucking child shall play over the hole of the asp,
>   and the weaned child shall put his hand
>   on the adder's den.
They shall not hurt or destroy in all my holy mountain;
>   for the earth shall be full of the knowledge
>   of the Lord as the waters cover the sea (Isa. 11:6-9).

That time is not yet, however. Ours is a day when our estrangement from God, from our fellow human beings, and from the nonhuman creation extracts a heavy price. The German biologist Friedrich Oelkers has put the matter in frightening words:

"For the animal and plant world, man is the very incarnation of evil itself. He is equipped with superior sinister powers. He goes around in all his ways according to his own caprice. He plants vegetation where and how he will and he destroys it again according to his pleasure. He modifies plant life according to his own shortsighted advantage because he possesses only a superficial knowledge of the laws of change and the vegetation follows him willing and still. The destruction, however, which man causes to the planet that has been entrusted to him is so terrible and at the same time so irreversible that in the long run in destroying the planet he must also destroy himself."[4]

It is clear here that humankind is of creation and suffers with nonhuman creation. Further, it is becoming clear to us that the whole of creation is caught in crises that are essentially beyond our power to solve. That is a hard lesson. It is a lesson, however, that may face us with our own limitations, the limitations of perversity and finitude, that we best recognize if we are to carry out the command to care for creation.

As sinful people, we tend to see problems to our own advantage. We take advantage of others and of creation in general in attempting to solve them. "Science is power," as Francis Bacon said at the beginning of the seventeenth century. He added that, through science, humankind could regain the proper domination over nature that Adam and Eve had lost in the fall. When this power is not used for service as Bacon intended, however, but for exploitation of both the environment and of people, it creates problems that outweigh the solutions achieved.

Finitude itself presents a problem. We know now that Nicholas of Cusa in the fifteenth century was wrong when he proclaimed the infinite universe as a proper correlate to the infinite God. We know, too, that Pierre Laplace was wrong when he saw the universe as a machine that obeyed inexorable natural laws.

For Laplace, the world was a predictable and precise machine. He postulated that, were there a mind that could know the exact position and velocity of any particle of nature, it could extrapolate the whole of nature both past and future from that one calculation. We know now, however, that nature is not subject to a consistent human rationality. It is something of a miracle that we understand nature at all. Jacob Bronowski has pointed out that our minds are not equipped to know reality adequately.[5] Physics itself has taught us that nature escapes our physics. Nature will always be beyond the ability of science to conceive it as it really is. The world inevitably escapes our observations, calculations, and even our imaginings. Both our concepts of reality and our calculations in its regard are, at best, approximations. They are useful, but they are never totally satisfactory. There is always more to know and the unknown may be rather different from what we imagine.

Historically, the two theories that have prompted the modern conversations between theology and natural science were Werner Heisenberg's principle of uncertainty and Niels Bohr's theory of complementarity. The principle of uncertainty shows that it is quite impossible to measure the momentum and the position of a particle at the same time. Precision in the one measurement stands in inverse proportion to precision in the other. Equally fate-filled as far as our knowledge in physics is concerned is the relationship between the measurement we select to make and the way nature shows itself to us. When we select to make one measurement, we *ipso facto* select not to make the other.

The crisis of knowledge arises because we are unable to know what half of the phenomena we are trying to take account of is doing while we are paying attention to the other half. Thus we are not able to envision the whole as a single picture. This means that when we "select in" any problem we desire to solve, we "select out" others that may be of equal import but that our selective processes prevent us from noticing, to say nothing of solving. We never see reality as a whole. We see the world as we have taught ourselves to see it.

We can be defeated, and we will be if we think we cannot be. We are finite and limited. More likely than not we delude ourselves when we seek grandiose solutions to the world's problems.

"The dream of the unlimited possibilities was a mad illusion. The technical world is a world of dreadful limited possibilities. The hungry millions will not be able to migrate to another star. The resources on earth are not inexhaustible. The faster the expansion of science and technology is driven forward, the faster it reaches its nontransgressable limits."[6]

The task of the church is to proclaim hope of redemption in the midst of crisis. As Christians, as those who have the fruit of the Spirit, there is hope in crisis. Our realization of the crisis itself is a sign of hope. In Romans 8 the Apostle Paul sets the whole of creation in solidarity with humankind in suffering as together all look forward to the salvation to come.

"We know that the whole creation has been groaning in travail together until now; and not only the creation but we ourselves, who have the first fruit of the spirit, groan inwardly as we wait for adoption as sons of redemption of our bodies (Rom. 8:22f).

For the Apostle Paul, creation along with the Christians who have received the first fruit of the Spirit (Rom. 8:23) groan, but they groan in eager expectation. Because Christians know of "the hope that is to come," they are signs of hope to the non-Christians and nonhuman parts of creation. Christians who participate in that hope are, therefore, the great promise for all of nature—the land, water, plants, and creatures.

"Creation hopes with eager longing for the revealing of the children of God . . . because the creation itself will be set free from its bondage and decay to obtain the glorious liberty of the children of God" (Rom. 8:19-21).

As Gerhard Liedke has pointed out, this "is a christological and pneumatological transformation of the *dominum terrae* of Genesis 1 and 9." This does not mean that spirit-endowed Christians redeem creation. Nonetheless, "by the way in which we Christians deal with suffering, the creation is shown how its hope stands, whether it is an illusion or not." If we aggravate the suffering of creation, human and nonhuman, hope sinks. If in suffering with creation, hope is expressed, then the suffering itself is reduced and "the creation's hope of freedom awakens to new life."[7] The eschatological hope of the resurrection is thus pulled into the present. Or rather it pulls the present toward it, giving hope to those who are children of God. Through them hope is given to all of creation.

This is what both Jewish and Christian apocalyptic literature is about. We are beginning to realize that the apocalyptic writers are not pessimists. Certainly they often speak of calamities, disasters, and catastrophes to come. The fact that they connect the fate of humankind (their anthropology) with that of the universe (their cosmology), however, shows that the literature has new relevance for us today. In the Book of Daniel the rulers oppress not only their subjects but the animals and earth as well. Mark 13 speaks of wars and rumors of wars. Brother will deliver up brother to death. Children will kill their parents. Tribulations will be followed by the sun being darkened and the moon not giving its light, even as the stars fall from the heavens. In the Book of Revelation the cosmic disturbances, the terrestial disasters, the plagues, the appearance of Satan, and the burning of Babylon set the background for the struggle of good and evil, Christ and Satan. Christ is victorious and judgment takes place. The wicked are condemned and the righteous rewarded. Then the new heaven and the new earth appear.

In the apocalyptic literature it is faithfulness in the crisis that is rewarded in the judgment. In that we live in a redeemed yet sinful world, our faithfulness is a sign of the hope of redemption that itself contributes to redemption.

The task of the church is to be first in faithfulness. How are we to be faithful? The answer to that question may determine our future and whether or not there is to be a future to determine. We may be faithful if we begin to realize that what we do to the earth, we do to ourselves. We may be faithful if we adopt life-styles that allow the advantages of science and technology to be spread abroad even if we can afford to keep it for ourselves. We may be faithful if we begin to see all particular problems as global problems, problems that affect everyone who is a member of the crew on the "spaceship earth." In the early days of space exploration, I once heard Buckminster Fuller give an address in which he said that whenever people would wonder out loud what it would be like to be on a spaceship, he would answer something like this: "Look around you. You are on one. Its name is earth. It is hurling around its main power station, the sun, at about fifty thousand kilometers per hour. It turns on its axis once in twenty-four hours with a surface speed of something over 16,600 kilometers per hour. We are all members of the crew."

Science and technology may be instruments of hope and means of being faithful. Science and technology, which we sometimes see as being responsible for "the mess we are in," are also responsible for the way we are enabled to continue to live and to interact with the world. Through a more rational and better use of science and technology they become a means of hope. Only through science and technology, which are continually being revised, will we be enabled to continue to survive and to attack many of the problems that plague the world.

We must be warned, however, that science and technology are ambiguous in that they are a part of the redeemed but still sinful creation. Some of the problems of the future will be caused by the very measures we take to solve the ones we have now. In that our solutions are, at best, partially adequate, we must be extremely humble and move with utmost caution.

But move we must. To stand still is to opt for disaster. The only solutions acceptable will be those that, according to our common best judgment, will benefit the world as a whole planet, including both nonhuman and human nature. Easy solutions are bound to fail. Selfish solutions, ones that are either personally selfish or nationally selfish, should fail.

Rather than give up the vision of solving our problems through science and technology, we must see science and technology as God-given instruments that, used correctly, extend our power for good. We need a bolder, clearer, all-inclusive dream. A dream that sees life and nature holistically. A dream that utilizes the best of historical, cultural, scientific, and technological imagination.

"For the earth is the Lord's and the fullness thereof, the world and all those that dwell therein; for he has founded it upon the seas, and established it upon the rivers (Ps. 24:1-2).

The task of the church in the new scientific age is, as is the task of the church in every age, to proclaim the gospel by word and act in such a way that the world might believe and be saved.

NOTES

1. Harold P. Nebelsick, *Theology and Science in Mutual Modification* (New York: Oxford University Press, 1981), p. 18.
2. Cf. "The Dialogue Between Theology and Science," Office of the Stated Clerk, The Presbyterian Church in the United States, 1982.
3. Lynn White, Jr., "The Historical Roots of our Ecologic Crisis," *Science,* Vol. 155, No. 3767 (March 10, 1967).
4. Friedrich Oehlkers, "Aus einer Rede, die der Biologe Friedrich Oehlkers 1957 auf dem Freiburger Universitaets-Jubilaum gehalten hat," cited by A. M. Klaus Mueller, *Die Praeparierte Zeit* (Stuttgart: Radius Verlag, n.d. [c. 1972]).
5. Jacob Bronowski, *Magic, Science and Civilization* (New York: Columbia University Press, 1978), p. 44.
6. Georg Picht, *Prognose, Utopie, Planung* (Stuttgart: Ernst Klett Verlag, 1971), p. 40.
7. Gerhard Liedke, "Solidarity in Conflict," *Faith and Science in an Unjust World,* Vol. 1, ed. Roger L. Shinn (Philadelphia: Fortress Press, 1980), p. 74.

◆6◆

How High~Tech Is Changing American Society

Judith K. Larsen

To name an aspect of contemporary life in the United States that has not been deeply influenced by technology is difficult. Business, manufacturing, distribution, labor, communications, transportation, health, education, government, entertainment, the arts, philosophy, religion—all have been changed by technological developments and their impact on society.

Indeed, this technology-based life is not limited to North America. People who have adopted a technologically-oriented way of life operate in nearly every society. Despite their diverse cultures, a radically different way of perceiving reality bonds these people around the world and sets them apart from others within their own culture. While they share language, race, and nationality with their geographic neighbors, they are part of a larger global community that recognizes the potential offered by technology and taps into the power of its information.

Whether technology's impact on individuals and society is a blessing or a curse is a topic of much discussion. Some observers see dire consequences in technology's advance. Others are optimistic, stressing technology's promise. As appealing as this debate may be, any consideration as to whether technology should influence society is outdated. Technology already has made a profound impact. Every part of the world has been touched, and social patterns and values have changed. This change sometimes gives the appearance of things falling apart, but in reality we are in the process of constructing a new society.

59

People have come to take technology for granted and to assume that it will always be there. As this assumption has become a part of their basic beliefs, they have adapted their behavior and attitudes. Their practices have shifted.

We experience it ourselves. We wear digital watches. We use calculators. We rely on instant communication. We expect high safety standards in planes, trains, ships, cars. We gain instant access to relevant information through on-line computers. We discuss international trade issues since they affect our "local" corporations. We respect people who are computer literate and people who keep up with current technological developments. Eventually our values and beliefs change.

Technology obviously cannot be treated as culturally neutral. It cannot be kept in a separate compartment, isolated from daily existence. It produces its own norms and refuses to be limited to those imposed upon it.

"Technology transforms human life and reason itself," Stephen Ross has written, "not merely changing the everyday conditions of thought and spirit, but producing a different world enriched by technological contributions. At a large enough scale, human activities transform the conditions of human reason, creating new spheres of production, fabrication and practice. We live in a different world today. . . . This technologically-produced world incessantly imposes new problems on us even while we engage in practice to control it."[1]

One of the problems that is especially pertinent to the church is that at the same time that technology-based subcultures are expanding, many people with traditional orientations are unaware of their existence. The gap between the technology-literate and the non-technology-literate is significant and is growing.

The first reason for this is that there may be no real need for the technology-literate and nonliterate to contact each other. It is possible, even likely, that their worlds do not overlap. Another reason is that problems of communication form a major barrier. Each group uses a different jargon language. To learn the language of the other group requires incentive. Thirdly, the lack of common experience limits the amount of useful dialogue that can take place.

Some technologists still believe that they are working on culturally neutral and value-free projects. Individuals who hold this view fail to see the relevance of discussion. Participation in dialogue makes no sense to them. In reality, the number of technologists who hold such a position is less than is popularly claimed. Yet even the technologists who accept the social implications of their work have few opportunities for nonsuperficial dialogue.

As technology's impact grows, the church should certainly be centrally involved as a participant in nonsuperficial dialogue. "The

Lutheran Church in America is called to acknowledge that it must express distinctively Christian truths in terms that are meaningful to the world around' us," the LCA stated in its *Call to Global Mission.* "Our ways of thinking about faith are often the product of a pre-modern age, while the world we live in is described in contemporary terms."[2]

♦ CHARACTERISTICS OF A HIGH-TECH SOCIETY ♦

If human knowledge and beliefs are largely communally determined, what is being transmitted in a high-tech community? It is not simply facts without values, or simply information. A technological "frame of mind" is increasingly recognized. How is it distinctive?

Several high-technology regions have emerged in the United States: Research Triangle in North Carolina; the Route 128 area around Boston; the Austin, Texas, area; upstate New York; Colorado Springs, Colorado; the Minneapolis-St. Paul metro area in Minnesota; and the Willamette Valley in Oregon.

Silicon Valley in California, however, is probably the epitome, even the caricature, of a high-tech region. It not only includes information workers but a relatively large number of people who produce the technology. More than half the work force is employed in high-tech industry. Findings here suggest trends likely to appear in technology societies throughout the world.

The most obvious characteristic is incessant change. Constant change in technology itself is a way of life. Technology depends on innovative ideas and new processes to sustain itself and to expand. Innovation comes from research, so research is the component common to all endeavors. It results in new ways of producing, manufacturing, packaging, marketing, and distributing. New products on the cutting edge may be truly unique, but only for a few months until a competitor brings out a newer version.

The pace of change in biotechnology especially has been astonishing. "In the late 1970s," Roger Schulman wrote in *Business Week* in 1985, "they first put human genes into bacteria, turning them into factories for useful proteins. In 1982, researchers altered the genes of a higher animal. Now scientists are about to take the next profound step—altering the genetics of humans."[3]

Change is obvious in the impermanence of products. Few companies make the same product now that they made twenty, or even ten, years ago. A chip that is two years old may be obsolete.

"High-tech industry is a place where every product is shortlived," an engineer told me. "I worked on the 1K RAM [semiconductor chip] when it first came out. We really sweated and sacrificed to develop that thing, and we were proud when it worked. But it didn't last long.

Now the only place you find one is in a museum. I worked on the 1K RAM and it passed. Then I worked on the 4K RAM. Now it's gone. Nothing lasts long. Things are always becoming obsolete. I've put in so much, but the products are gone. I have a sense of futility. Now I can see that there is satisfaction to be gained by putting energy into something that will last. That's why I'm working on my house. I'm making a mantel for my fireplace with stonework. That will still be there in ten years. I would like what I do to last."

Employers are only temporary. Companies are constantly starting up, growing, merging, being acquired, and fading away. A common characteristic of these companies is their small size. More than two-thirds of the approximately six thousand companies in the Silicon Valley have from one to ten employees, and eighty-five percent have fewer than fifty personnel. Only fifty-four electronics companies have more than one thousand employees. Most companies have a life span of under ten years. They are formed, grow, go public, are acquired, lay off employees, and dissolve. Few of the pioneer companies are still in existence. Employees who are laid off find that there is no company to go back to.

Another evidence of impermanence is the obsolescence of employees. The rate of job turnover is about thirty percent annually among professionals. This means that the average high-technology professional will have three different jobs in a ten-year period. Some claim that after seven years the technological education provided by a university undergraduate curriculum is obsolete. After that time it is up to the engineer independently to stay current.

Perhaps the most frightening evidence of constant change is the impermanence of personal relationships. Usually people in traditional societies depend on their jobs and their families or household members to provide support during times of transition. In Silicon Valley this support is frequently lacking. A high divorce rate and the acceptance of alternative life-styles are indicators of change. Fewer than one-third of the workers live in a "traditional" family composed of father, mother, and children. New family forms are emerging, often without intention or planning. Examples include families composed of self and children, self and spouse with no children, and self living with related and nonrelated persons. To underscore the rate of household change, a third of Silicon Valley's technology workers expect their living arrangement to be different within six months.

Single parents are usually also working parents, and as such they face special problems of time. Technology demands commitment and long hours from employees. A recent study found that half of the working mothers and three-fourths of the fathers spend less than two hours a day with their children. Many people find that their personal lives fail to provide a dependable base.

When knowledge is the raw material of a society, the extent of one's knowledge and one's capacity to absorb and integrate knowledge are key. Knowledge-based performance is the most valuable commodity. Success is based on the merit of the individual's work.

Knowing the technology and how to use it are the most important skills. It's not who you know, or who your parents are, or where you went to school, or what clubs you belong to, or any other social characteristic. It is what you know and how you apply it.

Meritocracy, with its reliance on knowledge and performance, is the positive side of this technology-based society. The sinister side is that one is left with few resources and little foundation when one's job disappears. Meritocracy can produce technocrats with limited life experience and with undeveloped fundamental beliefs.

The third characteristic of a technological society that I want to mention is one that is found throughout all industries and all regions of the United States. It is conscientiousness and creativity.

Most technologists received formal training in science and engineering, developing a mindset consistent with that training. For some, their academic training blended with curiosity and drive to produce an invention, an innovation, or an entrepreneur. For others, formal engineering training provided the foundation for a solid, and probably rewarding, career.

Solid technologists form the backbone of the microelectronics industry. Efficiency and rationality are important values for them and for the companies that employ them. Technology-based corporations, like most corporations, exist to achieve rational, materialistic, and economic goals. Most engineers in the technology-based society also hold these goals as important. Many mold their belief systems to be congruent with these values.

There is, however, another type of technologist—the technologist with vision. These are the creators of new technologies, new companies, and new industries. The thrill of creation drives these high-technology inventors just as it does creators in any field. They know the "high" that comes from working on state-of-the-art problems. Nontechnologists often overlook the creative aspect of the endeavor. They may even denigrate technologists who are focused on one topic, especially when that topic does not seem important to the observer. A major aspect of technological creativity that is distinctly different from its ability to confer status is its existential pleasure.

"Existential feelings," Samuel Florman writes, "are those irrational feelings that arise out of the depths of our innermost being— our intuitions, our basic impulses, what we feel in our hearts (which as Pascal said, has reasons that reason cannot know), in our bones, and in our gut. Engineering is an activity that is fulfilling existentially. . . . Our work often contributes to the well-being of our fellow humans. Every great engineering work is an expression of . . . purpose which cannot be divorced from religious implications. . . . Every man-made structure, no matter how mundane, has a little bit of the cathedral in it, since man cannot help but transcend himself as soon as he begins to design and construct it."[4]

◆ HIGH-TECH SOCIETY AND THE CHURCHES ◆

Major U.S. institutions—the family, schools, courts and legal system, labor unions, political parties, and not least the church—face a crisis of confidence. As new conditions emerge, institutions that once served well may become remarkably impervious to change. Then people begin to sense that their institutions are ignoring their needs.

One factor that limits contact between high-tech society and the churches is the way leadership in each group sees things. Technologists live and work in an environment that is constantly reforming to incorporate new findings. The churches rely on tradition.

Another problem is the tunnel vision that characterizes both groups. Many technologists fail to consider adequately the impact on society of the advances they produce. Their interest is concentrated on their technical virtuosity in the lab or the company or the factory. They usually have little awareness of the philosophical, social, and political implications.

Church leaders are the same. Many are unaware of the extent of the technological revolution that is taking place around them. They do not deal theologically with the implications. Many fall back on the plea that they know little about science so how can they be expected to contribute to an issue that is so foreign to them.

The limited contact between technologists and theologians leads inevitably to a misunderstanding of the basic messages, truths, and teachings on each side. Misunderstanding leads to confusion. Confusion, if not clarified, can lead to hostility.

In my own personal effort to clarify confusion and avoid hostility, I have identified five issues that are important to a technology-based society and three issues that are important to the churches.

The first issue is the spiritual crisis among technologists. This crisis is not particularly acute among technologists who do not understand the implications of their technology. They follow prescribed rules, truths, and procedures of science just as they follow prescribed rules, truths, and procedures of religion. But a minority of technologists, small in number but great in influence, do realize the potential impact. They are the innovators and entrepreneurs, people who bring a vision to their work and who consistently see its promise. Technology does not form a boundary for these people. Instead they match technology to a challenge. The technology innovators are today's folk heroes with their successes measured in dollars.

The less-known challenges confronting the technology innovators are questions of faith. Their response to the challenge is to acknowledge their spiritual crisis.

The second issue, from technology's side, is the church's view of technology. Most pastors continue to hold a modern world view in which technology is seen as an impersonal, detached, and objective search for the facts. They assume that all technologists come with a belief in the validity of hard facts. The familiarity with relativity and quantum theory in physics and evolutionary theory in biology, however, have led the thinking technologist to conceptualize the world as a dynamic connection of relationships, with reality being both actual and potential at the same time.

The third issue is the church's lack of pertinent theology. Technologists who have experienced a spiritual crisis and approached a pastor often come away disappointed. The pastor is not able to provide ethical and spiritual guidance on problems that are important to the technologist. The lack of theological direction represents a personal loss to the technologist. The defection of technological innovators results in a loss for the church as well.

The fourth issue is that the churches are seen as putting institutional interests ahead of the gospel. The responsibility of any institution is to preserve itself. This is well known to any technologist who has had experience with educational institutions and the government. Perhaps it is unrealistic to expect religious institutions to operate differently.

The fifth issue is the reluctance of the churches to tolerate a rich multiplicity of beliefs. The growth of technology has been possible only by pulling information and resources from a broad variety of disciplines and traditions. On the one hand are the backbone technologists who follow rational and normative practice and do not want divergent sets of values distracting them from what they are sure is truth. Their life course is based on a conventional wisdom that is designed to minimize ambiguity and the debate it can lead to. By contrast, the minority of technological innovators recognizes that all knowing is based on social relativity and history. These people wonder why theological pluralism cannot be accepted.

Now I would like to indicate the issues that I have identified as being important to the churches. A review of the position papers adopted by the churches on science and technology reveals that the concerns of the churches are not the same as the concerns of scientists and technologists; the gulf between the two goes on.

The first issue is humankind's relationship to nature and the cosmos. Many of the church statements treat science and technology as synonymous with the creation story. Discussions of science and technology end up being reviews of creation and evolution. Science and technology include more than biology and evolution. Indeed, quantum physics and relativity are much more important to major areas of microelectronics technology than are biology and evolution.

My second issue of the church is skepticism over the allure of science. The church's interpretation of the usurptive role of science and technology was probably accurate in the past when many hoped that technology could answer social, political, and economic needs. Indeed, even in the present many backbone technologists may continue to align themselves with classic technological values and beliefs. Yet as the realization grows that technology-based hopes were only dreams, the thoughtful observer realizes that technology's allure is powerful for technological innovation, not for addressing personal and social needs.

My final issue is that faith is essential to both technology and religious belief. The need for faith is one topic that both the churches and the technology innovators agree is critical.

"Science depends fundamentally on human powers of perception, recognition, discrimination, and interpretation," John Ziman has written in his book *Reliable Knowledge*. "The scientist as observer or communicator is an indispensable element of the knowledge system. But these powers have not been stimulated by an artificial, non-human device: there is no computer program, no formal algorithm, no string of logical operations to which these processes are equivalent or to which they can, in any practical sense, be reduced. Therefore—and this is one of the most important characteristics of the consensibility model of science—scientific knowledge cannot be justified or validated by logic alone. This proposition—anti-positivist, anti-inductionist—is now well entrenched amongst philosophers of science even if it is not yet universally accepted."[5]

Our understanding of the Christian message has always been related to our understanding of society. Even in cases of sudden upheaval, such as the Reformation, the Christian message proved to be malleable yet vital. We may be in an analogous situation today. The nature of the technology-based society calls into question some of the assumptions about society that have served as a philosophical foundation for centuries. The drastic changes now occurring in technology-based society require that if the Christian message is to be relevant to this society, new ways of conceptualizing society and the relationship of Christianity to society are needed. As we reconsider the nature of human social existence, we need at the same time to reconsider the meaning of the gospel.

The entire body of doctrine and theories, assumptions and prejudices of technology and theology must be the subject of dialogue.

Both technology and theology are at a decision point that could lead to great breakthroughs. The choice that each makes will set the direction for the future.

NOTES

1. "Technology and Practical Judgment," *Logos* 77 (1986).
2. *Call to Global Mission* (Lutheran Church in America).
3. Roger Schulman, *Business Week* (1986).
4. Samuel Florman, *The Existential Pleasures of Engineering* (New York: St. Martin's Press, 1976).
5. John Ziman, *Reliable Knowledge* (Cambridge; England: Cambridge University Press, 1978).

·7·

Genetic Engineering: Our Role in Creation

Ronald Cole-Turner

Most of us are aware of the changes genetic engineering is bringing into our world. For a number of years, churches and individual Christian scholars have commented on these developments, usually with a tone of guarded optimism about the potential for good that this technology possesses. Generally, these religious comments have been focused on the ethical issues of risk, control, use of human research subjects, and equitable distribution of benefits. All of these are important issues that require further attention.

Rarely, however, has there been extended theological reflection on the meaning of genetic engineering and on the ways in which it changes our basic relationship with the Creator and the rest of creation. J. Robert Nelson accurately describes the situation:

> "Christian theology has no ready-made solutions to the prob-
> lems being posed by the sudden advent of genetic engineering.
> There has been insufficient time for theologians to understand
> and assess the issues. The untimely expression of categorical
> judgments must be regarded with caution. . . . Yet the challenge
> to theology is an urgently demanding one."[1]

I want to explore this theological question. My belief is that a better understanding of the theological significance of genetic engineering will make it possible to articulate more clearly and persuasively an ethical vision of its use.

Before proceeding further, however, it will be helpful to think for a moment about how to reflect theologically on technology, and to look at a historic model of such reflection. The task of systematic theology, as I see it, is to bring the insight of the Christian tradition to the broad range of contemporary experiences. Under the Christian tradition, I would include primarily Scripture, and principally its witness to Jesus of Nazareth as the Christ; but I would also include the theology and the life of the Christian church through the ages to this moment. All this stands as a resource behind us, and to be a Christian theologian is to have one foot firmly planted in this tradition. To step outside that tradition is to cease to be a Christian theologian.

But the other foot must be extended to the broad range of contemporary experience, under which I would include personal and social experiences as well as the fruits of disciplined study. When the Christian tradition is brought into relation with contemporary experience, systematic theology begins. It is important to notice that in this way of thinking, systematic theology does not arise within the Christian tradition itself, but only in between the tradition and the world.

The range of experiences and disciplines is unlimited; our task as Christian thinkers is to relate all things to God. In North America, theology often occurs this way, but the principal partners in conversation for theology have been the disciplines of psychology and sociology, giving theology a personal and pastoral emphasis. On other continents, sociology and political science have been more directly engaged, giving theology a more political emphasis. Both of these are proper expressions of the theological method endorsed here. What has generally been neglected, however, is theological engagement with science and technology.

When the Christian tradition is brought together with some aspect of contemporary experience, often what we notice first is a clash or a dissonance. Christian tradition and contemporary experience often make conflicting claims or moral demands. As we seek to resolve this, we may find that the Christian tradition judges popular conceptions of contemporary experience perhaps as trivial, short-sighted, or self-centered. In this way, we find our lives and our thinking deepened and enriched by our commitment to this historic community of faith. Sometimes, however, contemporary experience judges the tradition as time bound or as conceptually limited in some other respect. There arises, in other words, a mutually critical juxtaposition of tradition and contemporary experience. It is in the middle of this critical juxtaposition that really creative theology occurs. And because contemporary experience continues to unfold with time, theology always has new reflective tasks and potential for significant new insight.

As we allow the conflicting demands of the faith tradition and contemporary experience to work themselves out in theological creativity, we begin to resolve them in new theological insight. Only at this point, I believe, do we reach a level of what is sometimes called "mutually critical correlation."[2]

Each time we achieve significant new theological insight, however, we need to ask how this new insight affects other areas of theological understanding. While no one thinks of theology as a highly structured system any more, it nonetheless aims at being a body of coherent affirmations. Major alteration of one aspect calls for a re-alignment everywhere else. For example, understanding human "fallenness" in evolutionary terms will call for a rethinking of what is meant by redemption and even of the work of Christ.

While traditional Christian theologians did not think of their work this way, more often than not they did in fact follow a method that resembles this. We can think of Augustine's response to the political crisis of the sack of Rome, or Aquinas's attempt to understand Christian faith in the light of Aristotle, or Luther's understanding of grace as transformative of human existence. If that is the case, then our task is not to repeat their content but their method. We must do as they did, not as they said.

An example of this might be seen even in the earliest sections of the Bible itself. The Yahwist text of the ancient Hebrews shows a remarkable adaptation of theology to a new context. As the Hebrew people made their way into Canaan, leaving behind a life-style of animal husbandry and taking up sedentary agriculture, they found the Baal and Astarte were the local deities, representing the very forces and processes of fertility upon which agricultural success depends. The people were tempted to leave Yahweh behind, for while Yahweh was a powerful deliverer from bondage in Egypt and a resourceful guide through the wilderness, the Baal and Astarte were the powers of fertility for agriculture. Could Yahweh be more than a god of rescue and pilgrimage and become a god of agriculture?

Notice how a technological shift poses the theological question. As they moved from pilgrimage and nomadic husbandry to sedentary agriculture, their old understanding of Yahweh was expanded so that Yahweh became the god of agriculture. We see this near the beginning of the Yahwist account where we read that "the Lord God planted a garden in Eden" (Gen. 2:8a). God became the proto-gardener or farmer at whose command humans were to be farmers and to cultivate and preserve the garden (2:15).

We know how the Hebrews divided the lands among the families and at least envisioned a periodic redistribution of the land, a kind of built-in land reform, to occur each fiftieth or Jubilee year. I cannot imagine that they would have thought this way without a theological understanding of Yahweh as god of agriculture. In other words, an ethical concern for a just distribution grew out of their theological vision.

A rough analogy can be found between the Hebrew situation and our own. Their technology of relationship to nature changed, and their theology changed with it. With the coming of genetic engineering, our technology of relationship with nature is changing, and I believe our theology should change, too. Like our ancestors in faith, we need to avoid the situation in which the new technology is outside the range of theology and therefore devoid of relation to God.

What is new in genetic engineering? We have discovered methods by which we can imitate natural ways in which genetic material is transferred from one organism to another, even across species. While this is not radically new in the sense that we are doing something that has never happened before in nature, we are now doing it quickly and intentionally. These two features—speed and intent— seem to me to be the principal novelties of genetic engineering. By imitating nature, we have acquired a new and growing power over nature.

If we believe, as many contemporary Christians do, that God has used these same natural processes over billions of years of evolution, and that through these processes God has created, then we must ask what, theologically speaking, we are doing. As creatures of evolution itself, we now direct a tiny fragment of evolution's processes toward our own purposes or intent. If God indeed has created through these very processes, and if divine intent has been working itself out through them and continues *(creatio continua)* even now, then how are we to understand our role?

To describe our role, some have suggested the term "co-creation." For instance, the 1983 report of the Panel on Bioethical Concerns of the National Council of Churches of Christ in the U.S.A. uses the term to refer to our use of genetic engineering. The panel affirms that "we are called to live in harmony with all of creation, including humankind, and to participate with the Creator in the fulfillment of creation."[3]

In a more recent statement adopted by the Governing Board of the National Council of Churches in May, 1986, the following is affirmed: "Creation by divine power is not static but dynamic and ongoing. As creatures uniquely made in God's image and with purpose, humans participate in the creative process through the continuing quest for knowledge, which now includes unraveling and learning to control the intricate powers compressed in genes of DNA molecules."[4]

While this report does not use the term "co-creation," it affirms the general idea, namely, that through genetic engineering, human beings have some role to play in God's continuing work of creation. Both studies affirm that genetic engineering opens the possibility of human participation, however modest, in God's ongoing creation.

Is "co-creation" a helpful term and concept to use in describing theologically the work of human beings in genetic engineering? I believe there are two conditions that need to be met before we can speak of the human role as that of co-creation: (1) we must have sufficient knowledge of the natural processes and the technical skill to affect them purposively; and (2) we must have sufficient awareness of the Creator's purposes to bring our human purposes into harmony with them.

We are rapidly meeting the first condition. Increasingly, we know how genes are moved from one place to another, and how they express themselves in the organism. We are developing a host of techniques to imitate the natural processes by which genetic material is moved around and switched on or off. Developments in this field have almost always come faster than predicted.

The second condition, however, is far more difficult. For if it is possible at all to discern the purposes of the Creator in the natural order, and in particular in the evolutionary process, this act of discernment will not occur in the genetics laboratory or among evolutionary theorists, for it is not accessible by these or other scientific means. Even the most advanced understanding of evolution will yield only a knowledge of the multifarious nature of the evolutionary process, with its conflicting and ambiguous tendencies and its dubious progress. No clear, coherent purpose is discernible, even with the most advanced science.

The conviction that there is, nonetheless, such a coherent purpose embracing the whole cosmos, including the evolution of life on earth, is (it seems to me) a faith affirmation, confessed because one stands in a tradition such as Christianity. It is informed by tradition, nurtured by worship, and expressed in personal commitment when we devote ourselves to serve this purpose rather than our own. It is not that the sciences contribute nothing to our understanding here. But it is crucial to begin with the recognition that the conviction that there is a single, coherent purpose to the cosmos arises religiously and not scientifically.

The sciences—and in this case particularly the theories of evolutionary biology—do help us understand more precisely the shape God's purpose takes in the world. For it is in this cosmos and on this earth that life unfolds, and if there is a God who summons forth life and gives it direction, this God works through the very processes best understood humanly through the sciences. These natural processes pose a material limit on what God can do. They do not reveal God's purpose, but they do say a great deal about the means through which God creates and the limits of the possibilities that are open to God.

The key point, however, is that Christian faith confesses belief in a God whose purpose transcends the processes of nature. In order to achieve this purpose, God is immanently present in the processes themselves, using them as an artist uses the medium of paint or as a poet employs words. But as we would not confuse the artist with the paint or the poet with the sound of language, so we must not confuse the Creator with nature, or God's purpose with the processes God uses in their achievement.

The ancient Hebrew Yahwist insists that Yahweh is not Baal or Astarte; that is, God is not fertility. But Yahweh is a god of fertility, working through biological processes to nourish and sustain human life within a natural order. Baal and Astarte are real processes but not independent purposes or deities. As real processes, they are subsumed under Yahweh's control and become instruments of God's work. God is not Baal or Astarte, or natural selection, or any other natural process, or nature as a whole. God is not nature,[5] but God works through nature to achieve a transcendent purpose.

By transcendent, I do not mean spatially distant, wholly other, or temporally removed into the future, but coherent. Nature itself lacks coherence. As its transcendent Creator, God gives to nature what nature lacks, namely a coherence of purpose. In giving this, God makes nature a creation. In other words, for nature to be a creation means that it is given a transcending, coherent purpose.

To the extent that we may discern that purpose, the way is opened for our technology to be used to cooperate with it. People of biblical faith have always felt they had some sense of God's purpose. The Bible speaks of many people responding to the prompting or the call of God and acting in specific ways in obedience to what they believed to be the will of God. These stories, however, are limited to the purpose of God in human history, and to human acts that cooperate with God in achieving this purpose. Now we are asking a related but nonetheless quite different question: Is the purpose of God in nature (in contrast to human history) knowable, and can we cooperate with it?

It is no puzzle why earlier generations did not think this way. For them, nature was essentially complete, and there was no outstanding purpose yet to be achieved in the arena of nature. While they may have believed in an unfulfilled historic promise of a reign of God yet to come on earth, the biosphere itself remained more or less a neutral backdrop. The realm of divine activity was human history. So was the realm of human activity; impact on nature was ignored or thought minimal.

Now, of course, all this has changed. We see God as engaged in natural creation, through evolutionary processes, even to the present. Further, we see our power to influence nature. And so we cannot avoid asking whether we are cooperating with God in achieving God's purposes in the natural world.

For these reasons, the term "co-creation" suggests itself.[6] Earlier terms, such as co-worker (*mitarbeiter* in German) or minister or instrument of God's will, are not rejected here, but something more is needed. These earlier terms seem more fitting when nature is seen as essentially complete. But if God continues to create, and if our work cooperates with God's ongoing creative work, then we need to consider the stronger term, "co-creation."

What can we say about our knowledge of God's purpose in creation? Theology has only begun to think this way, and our traditional Christian symbols have usually been translated in historic rather than natural terms. But is it possible to think, for instance, of Jesus Christ as revelatory of God's purposes in nature as well as in human history?

The prologue of the Gospel of John speaks of Jesus as the incarnation of the divine Logos, thereby linking Jesus with creation, not just with human history. The Logos is the principle of creation through which God creates all things. Over the centuries, Christian theology has seen Jesus Christ as the expression, within creation, of the Logos or divine structure of the creation itself. When the creation was viewed as essentially static, the Logos was seen as its eternal structure. In our age, it would make more sense to think of the divine Logos as divine purpose, not as that which gives eternal structure to the cosmos but as that which guides its physical and biological evolution.

The Christian conviction is that this Logos—or as we are speaking of it here, this divine purpose—is incarnate in Jesus of Nazareth, and that in his life we see made manifest, as far as possible within the compass of a single human life, the character and purpose of God. To the extent that it is possible to know Jesus as the Christ of God, it is possible to know something of God and of God's purposes, both for human history and for creation. Jesus Christ is not a fixed point binding us to his moment in our past, but a pointer opening the human future and showing us even now how to devote our work in service to others and to creation.

To know Jesus as the Christ, however, is not an abstract or theoretical kind of knowledge, but is born of grace and nourished through a commitment to discipleship, to participation in worship, and to the lifelong prayer that our lives will become formed in Christ. It is only as we open ourselves to being formed by God's purpose that we become aware of what it is. God's purpose is known only as it rearranges our lives. As our lives become formed, so then may our work become more informed by a conscious commitment to serve the purposes of God.

It is not natural for us to want to do this, and accordingly I am not inclined to think that much of our work is intentionally cooperative with God's work. And more to our point, I am not optimistic that much of what will happen in the future in genetic engineering can be dignified theologically with the label "co-creation." It will have an increasingly greater impact on nature, and it will serve human purposes, some individual, some corporate, some national, and some for all humanity. But rarely will we stop to ponder how our work fits into a greater purpose.

Earlier, I suggested two conditions that need to be met before we can speak of genetic engineering as co-creation. The scientists have, in recent years, succeeded wonderfully in meeting the first of our two conditions, that of understanding natural processes and developing techniques to alter them purposively. But we have not come nearly so far in meeting the second condition, namely a discernment of the ways in which this technology can be put to the service of God. We are, however, moving in that direction, and church groups are making the effort to understand this technology and respond to it with care and theological insight. More important, though, is the nourishment of the faith and vision of scientists within our communities of faith. To the extent that those who engage in genetic engineering are able to see their daily work as an expression of their Christian faith and as an act of obedience in response to their vocation, then God in grace might use their work as co-creative.

NOTES

1. J. Robert Nelson, *Human Life: A Biblical Perspective for Bioethics* (Philadelphia: Fortress Press, 1984), p. 158.
2. Cf. David Tracy, "Theological Method," in *Christian Theology: An Introduction to its Traditions and Tasks,* 2d ed. rev., ed. Peter C. Hodgson and Robert H. King (Philadelphia: Fortress Press, 1985).
3. Panel on Bioethical Concerns, National Council of Churches of Christ in the USA, *Genetic Engineering; Social and Ethical Consequences,* ed. by Frank M. Harron (New York: Pilgrim Press, 1984), p. 24.
4. National Council of the Churches of Christ in the USA, "Genetic Science for Human Benefit," pamphlet. 1986. Pages 14-15.
5. James Gustafson, who quotes John Calvin to the effect that "it can be said reverently, provided that it proceeds from a reverent mind, that nature is God," holds God and nature more closely together than I wish to. This quote appears in each volume of Gustafson's *Ethics from a Theocentric Perspective* (Chicago: University of Chicago Press, 1981 and 1984), pp. 258 and 36 respectively.
6. A. R. Peacocke uses "co-creation" and the even stronger term "co-explorer" to describe the human role, equipped by science and technology but nurtured by faith, in reference to God's ongoing creative work; cf. *Creation and the World of Science,* The Bampton Lectures, 1978 (Oxford: Clarendon Press, 1979), pp. 304-306.

·8·

Asian World Religions and Post-modern Science

Naozumi Eto

Asian world religions have little to do with modern science, which has been developed in the West and the North. Although some of the most important scientific achievements in world history have taken place in Asia (the invention of paper, gun powder, and compass through the genius of China; the discovery of the notion of zero in old India; and the great development of chemistry in the Islamic world), we must acknowledge that modern science is essentially a part of Western civilization.

There is no question that modern science and technology have greatly benefited the entire world. This giant, however, will become a gigantic devil and not be our gigantic angel anymore if it is allowed to walk around as it wishes without the control of genuine human wisdom. We can never forget the indescribable tragedy caused by the atomic bombing of Hiroshima and Nagasaki.

Nor can we forget such other tragedies as what is called Minamata disease. Minamata disease was more than a mere chemical accident. A chemical enterprise located in the remote city of Minamata on the southern island of Japan continued draining organic mercury from its factory into Minamata Bay for years. Many of the fishermen and their families in Minamata became paralyzed because the organic mercury condensed in fish affected their nerves. It even damaged the brains of fetuses in their mothers' wombs. Babies were born with brain paralysis and suffered greatly as they grew. What made the story worse was the fact that it took so many years for the company to compensate the innocent victims.

76

The reason why I don't—and won't—forget this tragedy is not only because I am from this island and not only because this was one of the first severe environmental pollution cases in Japan. I don't—and won't—forget this tragedy because it demonstrates the potentially terrible effects of modern science and technology if great efforts are not made to reconcile them to human beings and nature.

Here we must ask ourselves whether it is inevitable that modern science and technology neglect human welfare even though they were originally meant to serve humanity. Or is it the case that modern science and technology, the typical example of which is nuclear energy, are always double-edged swords one must handle very carefully?

These questions lead us to explore the very nature of, and philosophy behind, the development of modern science and technology that began in Europe in the late fifteenth century. What is characteristic of the philosophical thought upon which modern science was established?

The seventeenth-century philosopher and mathematician, Rene Descartes, based his view of nature on a fundamental division into two separate and independent realms: that of mind *(res cogitans)* and that of matter *(res extensa)*. This Cartesian dualism allowed scientists to treat matter as dead and completely separate from themselves, and it allowed them to see the natural world as a multitude of different objects assembled into a huge machine. Such a mechanistic world view was held by Isaac Newton, who constructed his mechanics on its basis and made it the foundation of classical physics.

This dualistic philosophy has continued to have a great influence on the general Western way of thinking right up to the present day. Descartes' famous *cogito* has been identified with mind instead of with one's whole organism. The mind has been separated from the body and given the task of controlling it.

This division and conflict between mind and body has become the division and conflict between subject and object within the individual. Each individual has been split up into a large number of separate compartments, and this "inner" fragmentation mirrors our view of the world "outside."

Though Cartesian dualism and the mechanistic view of the world greatly encouraged the development of classical physics and technology, they have also been responsible for many adverse consequences suffered by world civilization. It is natural, therefore, to try to overcome this fragmentation and return to the idea of unity expressed in Eastern philosophies as well as in early Greek thinking. Since the Eastern view of the world can be characterized as organic, wholistic, and ecological, such Western thinkers as David Bohm, Fritjof Capra, and Wolfgang Pauli have become deeply interested in finding harmony between the basic elements of the Eastern view of the world and those of the world view emerging from modern physics.

When we speak of the Eastern view of the world we are surely thinking of the Asian world religions.

In this paper I shall first attempt to describe the chief characteristics of modern physics, which is one of the fronts of what is called "post-modern science," and then I shall explore how and in what sense Eastern religious traditions are related to post-modern science.

◆ CHARACTERISTICS OF MODERN PHYSICS ◆

Science and technology are too often regarded as something neutral: Everything depends on who uses them. It is clear, however, that science and technology do not develop independent of a philosophy with which they are intertwined. Classical physics would not have developed as it did if it had been separated from the philosophy established by Descartes. With the development of post-Einsteinian physics a new philosophy or intellectual paradigm is required.

In classical physics, questions about the essential nature of things were answered on the basis of the Newtonian mechanistic model of the universe that reduced all phenomena to the motions and interactions of hard, indestructible atoms. Newton's equations of motion played a decisive role as the basis of classical mechanics. In his view, God had created, in the beginning, the material particles, the forces between them, and the fundamental laws of motion. In this way the whole universe was set in motion, and it has continued to run ever since like a machine governed by immutable laws.

It is clear that this mechanical view of nature is closely related to a rigorous determinism. The giant cosmic machine is completely causal and determinate.

In contrast to modern physics, the philosophical basis of this rigorous determinism was the fundamental division between the "I" and the "world" introduced by Descartes. At that time it was believed that the world could be described objectively, that is, without reference to the human observer. Such an objective description of nature became the ideal of all of the sciences.

In the twentieth century questions about the ultimate nature of matter have been experimentally tackled. The existence of atoms has been verified. Their constituents—the nuclei and electrons—have been discovered. And finally, the components of the nucleus—protons and neutrons—along with many other subatomic particles have been identified.

At the very beginning of this century Albert Einstein initiated two revolutionary trends of thought by developing his special theory of relativity and by investigating electromagnetic radiation in a new way that proved fundamental to the development of quantum theory. The whole situation in physics was radically changed. All the principle concepts of the Newtonian world view were shattered on the sub-atomic level.

According to relativity theory, space is not three-dimensional and time is not a separate entity. Space and time are intimately connected and form a four-dimensional "space-time continuum." In relativity theory, therefore, different observers will order events differently in time if they move with different velocities relative to the observed events. The Newtonian concepts of absolute space and absolute time as the stage of physical phenomena have been abandoned.

Quantum theory, on the other hand, demolishes the classical concepts of solid objects and strictly deterministic laws of nature. Quantum theory demonstrates that the world cannot be decomposed into independently existing units. In other words, quantum theory posits a basic oneness of the universe.

Niels Bohr's contribution was to develop the concept of "complementarity," which allows contradictions in interpretation of phenomena such as wave and particle, location and quantity of motion, energy and time.

Some striking ideas and paradigms have subsequently been introduced in the effort to develop a world view consistent with post-modern science. First, let me mention Karl Pribram, a brain surgeon who has specialized in the mechanism of memory. In his research he learned that damage to the part of the brain that is supposed to control the function of memory does not, in fact, destroy all of an individual's memory, although memory function is lessened to some extent. This finding has inspired him to posit that memories found in one location in the brain are not limited to that location, but rather that each part of the brain has a memory of the whole. He has dared to adopt a "holographic" model that has had nothing to do with brain physiology to explain the mechanism of memory in the brain.

Holography is a way of taking pictures of an object, without using a lens, through the use of equipment that produces a three-dimensional image. It is interesting that each part of the hologram contains or enfolds information about the whole. Here the reductionist principle that the collection of the parts recomposes the whole cannot be adopted. Pribram's hypothesis is that if the world is a gigantic hologram, then a brain is a point of a center of the world that deciphers potential information in the hologram.

David Bohm, who worked with Einstein and contributed to the formulation of quantum physics, has proposed a unique double image of the world that, to use the terms he coined, can be described as "Explicate Order" and "Implicate Order." The former is an order that can be recognized by three-dimensional measurement, but the latter is a hidden order that cannot be measured by ordinary means.

Bohm uses the hologram as an analogy for this Implicate Order because of its property that each of its parts, in some sense, contains the whole.

In summary, we can recognize that the development of modern physics requires of us a new intellectual paradigm that can overcome subject-object dualism and posit a fundamental oneness or harmony of all things in the universe.

I believe that this is not only a necessity on the theoretical level, but also on the level of praxis. The two examples I mentioned at the beginning of this paper (the holocaust by atomic bombing in Hiroshima and Nagasaki, and the terrible tragedy of Minamata disease resulting from the chemical pollution of the ocean) are to me concrete examples clearly demonstrating the need for a new intellectual paradigm on the level of praxis. They are not merely careless accidents caused by human sin.

Now let me explore how Eastern religious/spiritual traditions can make a positive contribution to solving the problems posed by post-modern science, including modern physics.

◆ EASTERN SPIRITUAL TRADITIONS ◆

A surprising parallel between the world view of modern physics and that of the Eastern spiritual traditions can be drawn. By the Eastern spiritual traditions, I mean Hinduism, Buddhism (especially Mahayana Buddhism), and Chinese thought (especially Taoism), and Zen. We are not interested in making clear distinctions between these traditions by pointing out details on the institutionalized religious level. Our interest lies in summarizing commonalities existing among the world views of these various traditions despite their diversity in appearances.

Hinduism, which represents the great civilization of the Indo-subcontinent, is a large and complex socio-religious organism consisting of innumerable sects, cults, and philosophical systems and involving various rituals, ceremonies, and spiritual disciplines, as well as the worship of countless gods and goddesses. In the ancient epic *Mahabharata* there is a spiritual poem called the *Bhagavad Gita* in which the god Krishna teaches. According to this spiritual instruction, the multitude of things and events around us are but different manifestations of the same ultimate reality.

The multitude of divinities are manifestations of divine reality. Each reflects a different aspect of the infinite, omnipresent, and ultimately incomprehensible *Brahman.* This *Brahman,* or reality, is understood as "soul" or the inner essence of all things. When *Brahman* manifests in the human soul it is called *atman. Brahman* and *atman,* the ultimate reality and the individual, are one. Through daily meditation and other spiritual exercises and yoga, union with *Brahman* is to be realized.

For many centuries Buddhism has been the dominant spiritual tradition in most parts of Asia, including Indochina, Sri Lanka, Burma, and Thailand through the Hinayana School; and of Nepal, Tibet, China, Korea, and Japan through the Mahayana School.

The Buddha is not interested in questions about the ultimate origin of the universe. Rather, he teaches the way in which one may free oneself and reach the state of total liberation called *nirvana.* To reach *nirvana* is to attain awakening or Buddhahood. In this state false notions of a separate self have disappeared forever and the oneness of all life has become a constant experience.

"Emptiness," one of the essential concepts in Buddhism for expressing the nature of reality, is not to be understood as a state of nothingness. Rather it is the very source of all life and the essence of all forms. By "emptiness" it is meant that all that exists in this world does not have substance. It also means that everything is set in motion and flows. Nothing ever remains the same as it is.

The *Avatamsaka Sutra,* which is regarded as the core of Mahayana Buddhism, was interpreted in China and Japan in a new way, and the philosophy of this school became the climax of Buddhist thought. The central theme of this highly sophisticated religious philosophy is the unity and interrelation of all things and events. This is the very essence of the Eastern world view.

We should also examine Chinese thought as represented by Confucianism and Taoism. Let me quote the Western writer Fritjof Capra, who rightly observes that "the Chinese, like the Indians, believed that there is an ultimate reality which underlies and unifies the multiple things and events we observe."[1] This reality is called *Tao,* which originally meant "the way." This is the way, or process, of the universe, the order of nature. In this original cosmic sense, "the *Tao* is the ultimate, undefinable reality and, as such, it is the equivalent of the Hinduist *Brahman* and the Buddhist *Dharmakaya.*"[2]

The difference between them cannot be overlooked. The *Tao* is different from the Indian concepts by its intrinsically dynamic quality. A principle characteristic of the *Tao* is the cyclic nature of its ceaseless motion and change. The notion of cyclic patterns in the motion of the *Tao* was given a definite structure by the introduction of the polar opposites *yin* and *yang*. The dynamic character of *yin* and *yang* is illustrated by the ancient Chinese symbols called *Tai-chi Tu* or "Diagram of the Supreme Ultimate."

Here we must note that the Taoist view that all changes in nature are the manifestation of the dynamic interplay between the polar opposites *yin* and *yang*. Any pair of opposites constitutes a polar relationship where each of the two poles is implicitly, but dynamically, linked to the other.

It is also important to realize that, according to the Taoist concept of change, change occurs not as a consequence of some force, but as a tendency innate in all things and situations. The movements of the *Tao* and therefore of the Taoist are not forced. They occur naturally and spontaneously. Such a way of acting is called *wu-wei* or "non-action," by which is meant refraining from activity contrary to nature. It is in this sense that Lao Tzu's words, "By non-action everything can be done," can be correctly understood.

Zen is a unique blend of the philosophies and idiosyncracies of three different cultures: Indian, Chinese, and Japanese. Yet Zen is purely Buddhistic in essence because its aim is none other than that of the Buddha himself, that is, the attainment of enlightenment, an experience known in Japanese Zen as *satori*. Zen is discipline leading to enlightenment. *Satori* means the immediate experience of the Buddha nature of all things. It follows that the perfection of Zen is to live one's everyday life naturally and spontaneously.

From this point of view, it is understandable that such arts as painting, calligraphy, garden design, and various crafts; such ceremonial activities as the tea ceremony and flower arranging; and such martial arts as archery, swordsmanship, and judo are all known in Japan as a *do,* or a "way," or *Tao* toward enlightenment. All these "ways" can be used to train the mind and to bring it into contact with ultimate reality.

◆ CONCLUSION ◆

Our efforts to illumine the common features among Eastern spiritual traditions has reached the stage where now we must examine the relationship between what is called "post-modern science" and those traditions.

Contemporary science and technology need a new direction, one that will overcome the limitations of subject-object dualism. It cannot be denied that this dualistic world view enabled the development of classical physics and underlay the scientific revolution. Yet something essential is missing: a philosophy that expresses the unity of all things in the universe as the ideal, purpose, and very nature of all science and technology.

Some people will respond by saying that it is not a matter of science and technology in themselves, but is rather a matter of who uses them and for what purposes they are used. From the very beginning, however, it has been impossible to divorce science from the prevailing understanding of the realities to which the terms god, human being, matter, nature, and universe refer.

We have also come to realize the serious dangers with which science and technology confront us. Besides nuclear weapons and the chemical pollution of our environment we face, for example, the problems created by genetic engineering, which includes genetic recombination. Such research should not be conducted apart from the development of a wholistic understanding of human being. A gene is not simply an object of medical science and technology. The manipulation of genes will eventually lead to the manipulation of other people as well as of oneself. I strongly urge the adoption of a wholistic view of human being.

One of our urgent but long-run agenda items should be to overcome the thought patterns based on the notion of absolute opposites. By this I do not mean that all things are equal. It should be recognized that the individuality of things must be affirmed while at the same time accepting that all differences and contrasts are to be taken as relative within an all-embracing unity. We are so accustomed to taking things in a black-and-white manner that we do not find it easy to assume an all-unifying reality beneath the surface.

If we can see beyond the world of opposites in science, we should also be able to see beyond the visible world of opposites. If we can overcome this dichotomy in our world view, it can also be applied to the world of science. In this sense, the contribution of the Eastern spiritual tradition will surely be great.

It is also interesting to consider the world in terms of the holographic model. Such thought leads us to see the whole not as a mere gathering of parts. It leads us, instead, to recognize each part as an essential factor containing all the information concerning the whole. Bohm's fascinating hypothesis of the Explicate Order and the Implicate Order is also suggestive in coming to grips with such a world view.

These and other new ways of interpreting the world receive interesting support from the results of scientific research. Ancient religious or spiritual world views and the new world view required by modern physics and other scientific disciplines seem to be resonating to each other. This congruence is quite helpful as we struggle to see anew the reality around us and in us.

I would like to pose a question that confronts Christians in our struggle to develop a new paradigm for understanding reality. Should we reconsider the concept of ultimate reality that in Christianity is designated by the term "God," a being who, it is believed, manifests itself in all things and events, and certainly in all persons? The traditional Christian concept of God, at least in its Western development, has been distinguished from the rather pantheistic concept of ultimate reality commonly found in Asian spiritual traditions.

In this respect, it is interesting to note that such process theologians as John Cobb have invested considerable effort in reconsidering the Western concept of God and that their efforts have led them into dialogue with Buddhism.

It would be fruitful to reflect on our traditional concept of God in the light of the new findings of post-modern science and in the light of Eastern religious traditions. We are encouraged to do this by our faith that God makes all things work together for good.

NOTES

1. Fritjof Capra, *The Tao of Physics,* 2d ed. (New York: Bantam Books, 1984), p. 94.
2. *Ibid.,* 94.

◆9◆

Scientific Research Is My Christian Vocation

Vincent P. K. Titanji

Inviting a biologist to speak of his or her Christian vocation is tantamount to asking how to reconcile biologic and Christian concepts of the world. For the committed Christian, science is a welcome and effective means of discharging a Christian obligation to serve others. It is in this sense that I see the pursuit of scientific knowledge as an expression of the Christian call to service.

My decision to dedicate my work to rural problems was probably influenced by my Christian commitment since I considered sharing to be one of the important aspects of Christian living. For the last nine years my activities have centered on (1) building an adequate infrastructure in Cameroon to do biomedical research at a sophisticated level and (2) looking for new cures for the debilitating disease known as river blindness. To these objectives must be added the effort to attract talented youngsters to deal with the problems of our rural masses, who are eighty percent of the population.

The disease known as river blindness is the world's most important cause of blindness. A poor second is trachoma. About 30 to 50 million people in the tropical countries of Africa and Central America are victims. In Cameroon alone, one tenth of the population of 10 million is affected. Up to six percent of these are expected to be blinded before they are fifty years old.

The parasite causing river blindness is transmitted from person to person by an insect, the black fly. It injects larvae, which look like snakes or worms, into the victim. One of our first tasks was to isolate this worm in living form so biological research could be done on it. One adult worm is about fifty centimeters long. During its lifetime it produces millions of microfilariae, which spread all over the body.

My good fortune was to return from overseas graduate studies just when the World Health Organization was about to set up a center for this disease in Cameroon. After joining the project we set the following objectives: (1) to develop a reliable diagnostic test for the infection since available tests were often insensitive, (2) to carry out feasibility studies for the development of a preventive vaccine, (3) to develop new drugs for the disease since known ones were either toxic or only partially effective, and (4) to attract and train young medical researchers.

Substantial progress has been made. Many of our original objectives are being met. We have developed a series of diagnostic tests against the disease that are currently being evaluated. Tools for studying the question of vaccination have been found. A number of plant products obtained from medicinal herbs in Cameroon are undergoing tests in our laboratories as potential new drugs against river blindness.

This last result arose from direct collaboration between laboratory-based science and the practical experience of herbal healers. We have succeeded in isolating the active ingredients in two Cameroonian medicinal plants. Compounds that are effective against the living parasite in the test tube are now being tested on laboratory animals. If our efforts succeed, they will illustrate how traditional medicine and modern science can collaborate in the service of rural communities.

While building up research facilities we have also developed a postgraduate program in immunology and biochemical parasitology. More than twenty trainees, some from neighboring countries, have successfully completed our courses. I believe that young Africans must take up the challenge of doing research relevant to our development needs. There are numerous difficulties, including the lack of funds and the lack of public awareness with regard to science as such. But ways can be found to advance the cause of science in the African environment. It is not sufficient for us to be passive consumers of science and technology. We must master and exploit it ourselves.

Earlier I mentioned that it is important for the Christian who is a scientist to find a means of integrating the Christian and the scientific concepts. For me this came naturally, with the Christian faith first and subsequently scientific training. There were, of course, times of inner conflict. These were mostly brought about by my incomplete understanding of both Christianity and science. As I grew older and understood better I came to see science as one way in which God reveals his magnificence to humankind.

Since I have been asked to be rather personal, I shall refer to experiences in my life that are relevant to living as a Christian and working in science. I came into contact with Christianity first through my parents and then, when I went to study in the Cameroon Protestant College (CPC), through the Basel missionaries. CPC offered a solid and broad training in both liberal arts and sciences. And none could go through CPC without acquiring a good knowledge of the Bible and Christianity. There the influence of the school's principal, a Swiss biologist, led me to choose a career in biology. I was fascinated that this man, with extensive knowledge in science, was a devoted Christian. As I was later to conclude for myself, scientific knowledge as such, and the knowledge of biology in particular, cannot automatically be the reason for accepting or rejecting Christianity.

This conclusion was strengthened for me while I was doing graduate study in the Soviet Union at the Moscow State University. At this point I shall not detail what it meant to live and study in the Soviet Union as such. I do, however, want to touch on those aspects that relate to the Christian faith while studying biochemistry in a country whose official philosophy is atheistic. Here I emphasize the word "official." At the time of my stay the university programs were deliberately designed to give the students what the Soviet philosophers called the materialist world view. Put succinctly, this world view asserts the primacy of matter over spirit. It is the theoretical basis for atheism.

Regardless of the subject of one's academic program, one was required also to take such subjects as economics, historical and dialectical materialism, the scientific basis of atheism, and the history of the Communist Party. These complementary courses were spread evenly throughout the entire degree program. In the case of biology they comprised about five to ten percent of the total load.

Soon it became known both among students and in the laboratory that, in spite of the impressive battery of antireligious information, many of us were still believers. This did not mean that we were insensitive to the information. We had to analyze it. I was surprised, for instance, that fifty years after the Bolshevic revolution it was still found necessary to convince Soviet citizens to be atheists.

According to their philosophers, religious beliefs arise from superstition and poverty. If this is true the Soviet accounts of economic development and advances in learning have to be faulty. Why was it still necessary to teach scientific atheism in the final year of the university curriculum? One Soviet philosopher admitted to me that every world view requires a primary article of faith, beyond which an internal logic may be developed. If this is true even for the materialist world view then it also must be true for the Christian world view. I saw no reason to change my faith since internally Christianity made sense to me.

After my graduation I went to Sweden to continue my doctoral studies. My arrival there coincided with a revivalist wave that was going through the Lutheran church. The warmth of Christian fellowship was a welcome change from my Soviet experience. I soon learned, however, that even the Christian Western society was not without problems for believers. The attitude of Western society seemed to be one of benign neglect of Christian faith and values. Social isolation, felt intensely by Africans accustomed to communal living, was for me an opportunity for reflection and self-examination. If in the Soviet Union I had stubbornly stuck to the Christian faith as a mark of defiance, here I had no need to do so. Churches were abundant but were often empty on Sundays. And religion was rarely a subject of social debate in the university departments where I studied.

During this period I had to reexamine my Christian commitment and redefine my priorities. I needed to clarify my attitude to the main question that biology poses to religion: the question of evolution as an alternative to creation.

Certainly, as with most modern biologists, I have no problem in accepting evolution. There is abundant supporting evidence. What I do not accept is that evolution necessarily excludes the action of God. Clearly the knowledge of biology, even at the molecular level, gives opportunity to wonder at the complexity and elegance of nature. It is amazing how a simple set of rules is used to construct organisms as complex as plants, beasts, and humankind. Each living organism has a genetic program, the DNA molecule, that is very similar in its physical properties from organism to organism, and yet so diverse in its information content. The principle here is to use a limited number of building blocks to construct a lone molecule bearing the genetic message. Whereas these building blocks are the same for each organism, the order in which they are placed along the chain and the length of the chains themselves vary from species to species, thus creating an incredibly large pool of information.

The same principle is used to construct proteins that are responsible for such manifestations of life as movement, the senses, growth, and excretion. Here, of course, the building blocks are amino acids.

I have described only two ingredients in the complex mixture of thousands of molecules that constitute the living cell. Nothing has been said of regulatory phenomena that put order in the complex reactions that take place within the cell.

For me it is simply unbelievable that all of this occurred of its own volition. Even if the writer of Genesis was inaccurate in his vision of the origin of life, in my opinion he had considerable insight. Not only was he able to recognize that life could not originate without light, he also recognized the necessity of water for the emergence of life. That is still accepted in the most sophisticated biological theories of our day.

I have come to believe that biology is not a good reason for me to abandon Christianity. Life is too complex. Life is too beautiful, too intelligently constructed to have happened all by itself.

In addition, there is the evidence of faith. But then faith makes sense only to those who already have it.

◆ REFLECTIONS ON SCIENCE AS VOCATION ◆

Ted Peters

Too often we have made the double mistake of equating the church with the kingdom of God and then limiting our concept of vocation to a call from or to the church. Even the church itself is called. The New Testament word for church, *ekklesia,* means "that which is called" from the world and to the world for the purpose of witnessing to God's kingdom in the name of Christ. When we are called to a vocation in science, we are called to work in and for the kingdom of God, regardless of whether it is inside or outside the church. Dr. Titanji's call to arm himself with the weapons of biomedical research in order to do battle against river blindness, I believe, constitutes such a divine call.

Dr. Titanji indirectly raises another issue: the role of science in the Second, or Communist, World. One of the major intellectual conflicts of the last century and a half has been between the left and right wings of the Enlightenment. The right wing Enlightenment has dominated the modern democratic West. Science in the West has been conceived as requiring the freedom to inquire in whatever direction the truth seems to be leading. Even if at the macro level Western researchers have become beholden to government and military patronage, at the micro level—the level at which scientists work from day to day—the research must be free and its conclusions potentially revolutionary. Otherwise it cannot rightly be called science.

The assumption of the left wing, in contrast, is that all intellectual activity is subject to covert class ideology and that science, in principle, is unable to revolutionize its patron class consciousness. Having made this assumption, a communist regime feels justified in replacing the alleged covert ideology with an overt state ideology and taking full control of the direction science follows.

In the future we need to study the role that freedom of inquiry plays in Second World societies. A study of this sort might yield a benefit for First and Third World churches, especially those that are tempted to give priority to ethical praxis over theoretical theology. Theoretical theology is being attacked right along with theoretical science. This is being done by those among us who, in the name of liberating the oppressed or preserving the environment, are willing to shut off dialogue with working scientists. They attack scientists who claim that their research is morally neutral. They launch this attack on the grounds that technology has allegedly perpetrated unmitigated violence on the Third World peoples and on the global environment. Religious leaders of this type fire merciless diatribes against modern science in the name of a Christian commitment to justice.

The problem here is that such attacks fail to discriminate carefully between science and technology, or between science and scientism. The worst case atrocities of modern technological destruction—which we all acknowledge as atrocities—are constantly trundled out as ciphers by which the whole of modern research is dismissed as diabolical scientism. The solution, such liberationist spokespersons suggest, is to subordinate theoretical research, both scientific and theological, to the prereflective praxis of the church. The net effect of such a position is an intellectual disaster. What we produce is a church that listens neither to the scientists nor to the theologians. How can we be surprised, then, when scientists look upon our religion as an atavistic danger to rationality and upon our church leaders as a fanatical danger to sanity?

Regardless of what we believe to be the intrinsic ethical and political ramification of scientific research, we in the churches need to open channels of communication and opportunities for mutual influence between science and our lives of religious commitment. We see the result of such communication in the person of Dr. Titanji. He is both a scientist who is fascinated by the search for truth and a committed follower of Christ who is dedicated to loving those who need his work in Central Africa. He has answered a call. He has taken up the vocation of a scientist in service to his faith.

·10·

Agenda for the Twenty-first Century

Robert John Russell

My task, at the end of this extraordinary conference in Cyprus, is to reflect on what I have heard and to suggest some directions for the church in light of these concerns.

◆ VOICES AND MANDATES FROM REGIONAL GROUPS ◆

Let me first highlight some of what I have heard while visiting the five regional groups during this week. In one form or another many of you have been concentrating on issues, including:

◆ the meaning of church mission in a scientific and technological age;

◆ the task of constructive theology given the challenge of contemporary science;

◆ the vocational challenge for Christian scientists seeking to relate their Christian faith and values to their research and discoveries;

◆ the call to solidarity with the Third World as it struggles under the impact on its culture produced by the massive importation of foreign technology, as it rejects the ideological element that all too often accompanies such technology, and as it moves to develop indigenous, appropriate technologies;

◆ the call to ministry to technologists whose lives are oppressed by the very technologies they produce;

◆ the call to solidarity with the church in the Second World as it struggles for a voice in an atheistic society; and

◆ the prophetic demand to oppose all forms of oppression and war empowered by new technology.

Your groups seem to be in general agreement on a number of directions for the future. You emphasize the importance of education, with special attention to teaching basic science and technology for clergy and theologians, and basic theology and ethics for scientists whose research poses ethical issues. You acknowledge the importance of developing indigenous technologies in the African, Asian, and South American regions, technologies that are economically and ecologically responsible and that can be owned and controlled by local community groups instead of national or multinational corporations. You suggest recovering and celebrating those indigenous African, Asian, and South American world views being submerged by the importation of Western culture via science and technology. You stress recognizing that each region has its own unique issues; addressing these issues through regional organizations; and sharing these issues and indigenous technologies through inter-regional conferences and networks. You recognize that there are some inherently global issues that transcend regional boundaries, which must be addressed through international organizations. And you urge overcoming the opposition by some churches to scientists who want to participate in their churches.

Still the overriding imperative I've heard (and it has come from each group) is the need for education, since the most important source of power is knowledge. And the knowledge we need comes from two books—the Bible and nature. Unfortunately the church and the scientific communities that have grown up around each book have somehow grown far apart, becoming two worlds unto themselves. Hence the education being called for by you entails learning to build bridges between these two worlds.

In view of these concerns, I have the following hopes for our road ahead. First, the First World needs to be healed from the ills of its excessive dependence on energy-intensive technology and non-renewable resources, and to turn its energies more fully to the support of basic research that truly liberates the human condition and lifts the imagination. I hope that the First World can reach out to Christians in the Third World for help in that healing process as more appropriate, more humane technologies are developed there and shared internationally, and as world views indigenous to the Third World, in which humankind and nature are often seen as interdependent and whole, are reclaimed and celebrated globally.

I acknowledge the charge that we in the First World tend to export scientism, of one variety or another, along with science. Many in the Third World are right to refuse our technology if its price tag includes the destruction of their world view and way of life, and if the only alternative is the materialistic world view we too often offer along with the technology. The First World needs to rediscover and construct a new world view broad enough to include science and religion, one with the ethical wisdom and force to help shape the development and use of technology for human and environmental betterment.

Second, the Third World needs to distinguish very carefully between competing claims in two separate areas: (1) Between Western science and the ideologies attached to it, exploiting Western science to Third World advantage while rejecting the ideologies as idolatrous. Basic science must be taken on board regardless of its cultural origins. In fact, it is the very transcultural character of science that can supply the best weapon against those ideological attachments, for they will be relativized and rejected as a new culture claims for itself the kernel of scientific truth. (2) Between those technologies, especially in medicine, food and energy production, and communication, that have universal value and those that finally enslave. As you recognize the problems the First World has encountered, you must work to avoid them for yourselves. Your leadership here could be of great help to the First World in recovering its own spiritual insight and moral direction.

Finally, I believe that the church is being called to a truly global mission involving four directions:

(1) We must act as educator, in which knowledge gained by science and gleaned from the Bible can infuse our common vision of the future. Scientific and religious knowledge is transcultural: neither the gospel nor quantum mechanics changes "as you cross the Equator" in either direction, if I may be permitted to modify that famous remark by von Weizacker. Certainly there are cultural influences and personal biases to both kinds of knowledge, and neither is absolute. Still the truth each contains is a genuine discovery about the world we are part of and the God who makes and redeems us all. Hence it is our common human right to share in and contribute to these kinds of knowledge. Since knowledge liberates by its power of truth, the church must be committed to its discovery and to its dissemination.

(2) We must act as a mediator between First, Second, and Third World cultures. We must sponsor theological and ethical research on the issues raised by science and technology and develop an international network to promote this research and education. Many of the technologies already in place in the First World are only now reaching the Third World, and this provides a unique opportunity if we act quickly. We can take advantage of lag time to encourage Third World countries to produce its own technologies, to prove that simpler often works better.

(3) The church must speak prophetically, keeping us all— First, Second, and Third World alike—from any idolatry, in which technology itself (or any other human product) is seen as ultimate (whether ultimately good or evil).

(4) Finally the church must empower us all to become ministers of the gospel, to be the priesthood of all believers. In this world of burgeoning technology, conflicting world views, staggering new knowledge, and remorseless oppression, we must become God's agents of forgiveness, of healing, of truth, and of liberation. To do this requires all three of the directions above.

◆ HOW WE GOT WHERE WE ARE ◆

To move ahead we need to recall who we are and what our history is, for we Christians above all are a people of history and story. Let us not forget that we have come to a conference like this over bridges that were built for us by pioneers for whom a conference like this would have been unthinkable.

Much of the groundwork began to take shape in the post-World War II period when science and religion were in totally separate worlds and there was little concern over the potential liabilities of what were then glittering new technologies. We owe special thanks to such pioneers as Paul Abrecht, Ian Barbour, and Arthur Peacocke, who laid the groundwork for the possibility of a conference like ours, and to the World Council of Churches in particular for its sustaining interest in these issues. Many of these scholars took advantage of a school of thought in the philosophy of science, namely "critical realism," using it as the bridge-structure across which methods and concepts in theology and science could be fruitfully exchanged. They often assume a philosophy of emergence, in which explanations of more complex evolutionary systems required new and irreducible concepts, insuring a degree of autonomy between the natural, social, psychological, and theological sciences.

The challenge these thinkers faced was twofold: reductionism on the one hand and compartmentalism on the other.

When scientists try to explain everything they can with a given theory, it is called methodological reductionism, and as such it is a legitimate research strategy. When they claim, however, that ultimately every other field of inquiry will be explained by their own field (usually physics!), it becomes epistemological reductionism. This would mean that psychology is "nothing but" neurophysiology, that biology is "nothing but" physics, that all the rest is mere appearance (that is, merely epiphenomenal). This in turn gives way to ontological reductionism, the belief that all there is to reality is "matter in motion," the inanimate stuff physics studies. Such a move would surely leave religion defenseless unless one turned to some form of dualism, such as separating body and soul, reason and faith, or mind and spirit.

Dualism in turn led to compartmentalizing religion and science, however, and indeed to compartmentalizing all fields of human experience and knowing. Sometimes these compartments were taken to be conceptual, sometimes linguistic, sometimes focused on distinctions such as subjective versus objective, reason versus revelation, or others. Scientists challenged religion as lacking empirical data, arguing that values are purely arbitrary, that preaching hasn't changed society, that there is no ultimate hope in a world where even the universe will someday die. Religionists in turn often attacked technology as the root of human oppression and environmental disaster, and retreated into spiritual, intellectual, and moral isolation, renouncing any effective role in social decision-making.

Theologians too had their reasons for defending a compartmentalist approach. Neo-orthodoxy, typified by Karl Barth, rejected the nineteenth-century compromise of Christ and culture, with its roots in Schleiermacher, and insisted instead on the radical separation of the Word of God and human discovery. Others such as Paul Tillich adopted an ahistoric existentialism in which nature played no substantive role in human experience. Finally, for those who followed Rudolf Bultmann the challenge was to extract the *kerygma* of the New Testament from its mythological framework, and to preserve it from the new myths of science by keeping the gospel uncultured.

Because of this a whole generation of pastors grew up in a "two-worlds" climate and the church grew increasingly insulated from and ignored by the intellectual history of its age.

In this and many other ways too numerous to recount here, each side of C. P. Snow's "two cultures" saw the other as pathetic, hypocritical, conceitful, arrogant, and finally irrelevant. Those who have led us to where we are now had to overcome both reductionism and compartmentalism by science and religion. They did so by envisioning a new form of continuity between science and religion in which both similarities and differences were maintained. To see them in terms of continuity meant asking three questions: What kind of knowledge is found in theology and in science? How do we obtain that knowledge? How do we express it? These are questions of epistemology, methodology, and language.

They stressed that there is indeed a process of consensus even within the religious community involving intersubjective testing. They argued for the role played by paradigms both in the history of science and in religion. They challenged us to think of Christianity as a paradigm or even as a set of paradigms. By analyzing religious and scientific language they pointed out the common role played by metaphor and showed us that models, as sustained, coherent sets of metaphors, are central components in scientific theories and theological doctrines. Using the work of Michael Polanyi, they have argued passionately that faith is a presupposition of knowledge in either field: both faith in the methodology of inquiry and in the underlying concepts of any specific theory. They have argued for wholism by using the very sciences, such as quantum physics, thermodynamics, and evolution, that have been cited in favor of reductionism.

Out of their work comes the picture of nature as emergent and with it an epistemology of emergent levels. This epistemology avoids both reductionism and the watertight compartments of isolated language games, because, though "lower levels" provide rules of consistency for "higher levels," they never erase their autonomy. I can't do something biologically that violates the laws of physics, but the laws of physics can never produce all the laws of biology.

The challenge to them has been to find ways to balance the assertion that we truly live in one world and yet understand it through a multifold epistemology. How do we know that all these fields "get at" the "same world?" How do we bring this "Tower of Babel" together? And more pointedly for us at this conference, what is the role of theology in the integrated system so produced? Is theology one more level among many, or is it committed to the integrative process of all the levels?

Finally, how do we know that we know something theologically and ethically about the whole, something that is useful and makes a difference to the whole, something that directs our praxis in the world? Who decides and who benefits from this knowledge? In short, what counts as progress in science and religion?

We are now moving, however tentatively, beyond dialogue into some form of mutual modification in which technology and values will play a significant role. And there the question is: How much can each side be modified? If theology can gain by interchange with science, can science gain by interchange with theology? Can the ethical challenge of technology force us to greater theological insights concerning fundamental science? Can such a theological renewal lead to sharpened ethical criteria for technological research?

It may well be that theology and science have each taken into their own conceptual systems pieces of the other, so that we really stand before two distant cousins, not two strangers. There may be inherent metaphysical, fiduciary, and aesthetic elements in every scientific theory: through its presuppositions and concepts, through its boundary questions, through its limit questions, through its sense of mystery, through its inability to ground itself, and through its a priori nature. There may be, on the other hand, elements of science in every theological doctrine, through the cosmologies assumed in its textual sources and the influence of culture on the history of tradition, through the very processes of reasoning, and through the collective formation of religious consensus that gives theology its own form of rationality.

And so today we are at a new point in the relationship between science and religion. I think it is very promising, and yet very challenging. Now that the bridges are being built we need to get on with the task before us. We must move across these bridges into the frontier beyond epistemology, methodology, and language to a real sharing of ideas and commitments about our universe and the God who is our Author and Redeemer.

♦ BRIDGES TO THE FUTURE ♦

As many of you have stressed this week, there is an increasingly large segment of society that finds the concepts and language of the church to be meaningless, principally because of its inability to speak to an age informed and influenced by science and technology. How then can the church have any significant voice in the world of the twenty-first century, if it is rapidly losing it today? Without credibility our prophetic voice will be lost. We thus face a whole series of questions that are long overdue and that, in my opinion, the church must address if it is to maintain its credibility and its prophetic stance in the twenty-first century.

Perhaps the most striking challenge is one that has surfaced several times this week, both in the lecture of Arthur Peacocke and in private discussions in the regional groups: How can God act in the world governed by the laws of science? Why do we need God if we can give an increasingly complete explanation of our origins, nature, and future in terms of science? Surely God acts in persons, communities, and histories, but can God act in the biological, physical, and cosmological dimensions of creation? In light of the natural sciences, can we once again recover the meaning of the immanence of God "in, through, and under" all the processes of the world while at the same time defending the transcendence of God with respect to all creation? Can we view all moments and events ultimately as God's activity, and if so, is God affected by the world as well?

How, for example, are we to understand God's relation to the universe as Creator in terms of contemporary cosmology, with its portrayal of the entire universe as emerging from a primeval Big Bang? By working with the discoveries of science, can we gain new insight into the relation of time to eternity, of space to God's omnipresence, of earth to heaven, of creation out of nothing to the absolute dependence of the universe as a whole on something beyond itself, and of continuous creation to the emergence of novelty and complexity within the processes of the universe?

What is the theological significance of the human species, including human origins, human nature, human social and moral behavior, human culture, and the human future, in the context of evolutionary biology? For more than a century the church has wrestled with Darwinian theory. Evolutionary theists have argued that God is at work in the biological processes that have formed us, but conservative wings of the church have remained committed to a literal interpretation of Genesis. How are we to respond definitively to fundamentalism without retreating to the "two worlds" solution-by-divorce? What constructive theological response can we give to evolution?

Moreover, we are learning that to be *homo sapiens* is to be *homo faber* or "tool-maker," as the Metropolitan Gregorios impressed on us so eloquently this week. Technology is not just the product of culture; it is the shaper and producer of culture. In a sense, it is culture. Given this perspective, the task of the church must be to help us choose the road ahead in light of the biblical norm of the lordship of God over all nature, including human nature. Ron Cole-Turner brought us the dramatic encounter between our biblical understanding of stewardship and the new genetic technologies being developed today. Is our traditional understanding of "tilling the soil" adequate for the ethical issues raised by medical and reproductive technologies and by genetic engineering, or are we to work under the rubric of "created co-creator," as Phil Hefner and others are urging?

Many believe we have within our reach the power to begin massively reshaping the biological environment, and perhaps even our own gene pool, through our increasingly powerful genetic and medical technologies. Hence we are at a point where the theological vision of human nature as *imago dei* and the ethical imperative to liberate humankind via the gospel as praxis merge in the morally ambiguous power of the technological future. The church must be prophetic in this cauldron of promise and crisis.

There are numerous other ways in which the natural sciences are playing an increasing role in other theological areas long thought to be far removed from them. We are beginning to see the role of chance as treated by quantum physics, thermodynamics, and evolution, in the theology of creation and in theological anthropology. Does God act against chance to produce order, or is chance catalytic to the generation of order? Is entropy in the physical world a sort of precurser to evil in human culture, or does it too play a role in the evolution of higher structures, the goals we value as life-giving and good? What is the relation of mind to nature, of free will to causal indeterminacy, of time's arrow and history? Cross-disciplinary insights arising from the interaction between the biological and the social sciences pose enormous challenges to the church. How strong a determinate is biological evolution in the rise of culture and its moral codes? Is altruism simply a strategy for the survival of the gene, or is the role of biology more that of a constraint on the emergence of new and irreducible phenomena at the level of culture and religion?

Science has vastly expanded our vision of the universe and humbled our "place" in it. We now know there are billions of stars in our galaxy and billions of galaxies spread across almost limitless space and time. How are we to understand God as Redeemer in the context of such a cosmic vision? If religious pluralism, cultural relativism, and inter-religious ecumenism challenge the Christian witness to the centrality of Christ in God's redemption of the world, how much more does the cosmic perspective of a universe teeming with sentient life! What meaning will we give to the problem of sin and the universality of the cross and atonement in the context of the universe around us?

Science has not only opened up a tremendous time scale in the past, it is also forcing us to think in terms of an incredibly extended future, one in which the sun and the earth will last several billion years and the universe at least 100 billion. In this context, what do we mean by bodily resurrection, eschatology, the parousia, or the fulfillment of history in the last days? Is Christ truly the cosmological alpha and omega? Yet even with such an overwhelming scale of time, the universe seems destined finally to end either in a violent blaze of infinite temperatures or to freeze in an unending expansion, continuing lifeless for countless eons.

The prospect of the death of the universe, of all that is, has loomed behind many of the greatest minds of our century, from Bertrand Russell writing so poignantly at the turn of this century, to Nobel laureate Steven Weinberg, who recently lamented, "The more the universe seems comprehensible the more it also seems pointless." Perhaps the biggest challenge from science is this possibility of ultimate meaninglessness.

In a profound way we are actually living in an age of spiritual poverty, an age sorely in need of the good news of God's presence and purpose. But our age, as any other, needs to hear it in a way that it can be heard. This is a fundamental challenge to the proclamation of the church—one we must meet, one merging with the struggles of peoples everywhere for both political and spiritual liberation. It is a challenge we must meet if we are to preserve the gospel for tomorrow.

Of course there are numerous other topics for research. One area is the meaning of revelation in an age of empiricism. How are we to understand the relation between reason and revelation? If the canon is, in principle, open, what are its sources, and can they include science? How indeed do we relate theological and scientific truth claims? Should our creeds, in the process of reformulation, be responsive to the world as we now understand it through science?

Another topic is the role of nature in our language about God and humankind. Can the language of nature be used effectively and inclusively in church documents and liturgy? Can we think of the earth, even the universe, as a sacrament? What power does prayer have in the world? What is the meaning of miracle?

The list of issues is endless.

♦ FROM BRIDGES TO THE ROUNDTABLE ♦

I've also sensed a striking change in this conference from the way science and religion were looked at before to the way you are telling me they are to be looked at now. I want to ponder that change for a few minutes, to look at its strengths and its liabilities.

The change involves two distinct claims. The first broadens the discussion to a four-way dialogue or roundtable; the second challenges the legitimacy of the dialogue as ultimately ideological.

The first claim is that, up to the present, we have seen theology and science as one pair of dialogue partners and ethics and technology as another, separate pair. This week many of you have urged that we need a new perspective in which theology, science, ethics, and technology enter into a four-way dialogue as four mutual partners. Such a new perspective, if it can be achieved, should clarify the agenda of the church as it struggles for justice, peace, and sustainability in a global context.

I am excited about this broadened discussion. While I continue to believe that clear support must be given for fundamental research on the conceptual challenges from theoretical science to church doctrine, the context of this research may well become the four-way interaction in which such conceptual issues are enfleshed in our lives and social structures by technology and the crises of values technology raises. To that end I have some specific suggestions I'll make at the close of this presentation.

The second claim involves the sociological and even ideological dimension of science. Though I discussed some of this material above, this challenge needs to be faced directly now. Does even fundamental science inevitably take on an ideological character then, so that even basic science cannot be seen as value-free or trans-cultural? And if it does, ought Christians freely engage in scientific research or promote science education without being concerned for its inherent ideology? This claim was given particular emphasis by several representatives of Second and Third World countries, and it reflects what some sociologists of knowledge are arguing in many parts of the First World as well.

These scholars certainly claim that indisputable social factors shape all forms of knowledge, including theoretical science. Yet even those who press this thesis do not mean that such knowledge is in any way less than just that—knowledge. These sociologists argue that the language through which knowledge is gained and expressed is inevitably linked to the indigenous culture. Metaphors are a prime example of the influence of culture in all human knowing. They are intricately related not only to the languages of the humanities but also to those of the sciences, as even critical realists who do not agree with the extreme sociology of knowledge thesis will argue.

Yet I would contend that the fact that knowledge arises within and through culture does not eliminate its universal character and its capacity for verisimilitude. Scientific theories are typically stated in universals. Without these transcultural claims they could not be considered scientific, if by this we mean capable of falsification. What good would a theory be if, whenever it were potentially disproven, the data were rejected out of hand as culturally biased and irrelevant.

The lesson we must learn, moreover, is that competition is healthy, even in epistemology. It is not that the First World should not propose scientific theories in universal language, but that it should welcome those proposals of the Third World as well. Theories from every culture should be put to the test. Moreover, many types of phenomena from the Third World may get systematically ignored because they don't fit into Western theories. Traditional forms of medicine, such as acupuncture, are clear examples of the wealth of data gleaned through centuries of human experience and craft that may well deserve a theoretical interpretation but that have had a very poor hearing in the West. In the long run it will be to the advantage of both First and Third Worlds if new theories can be advanced as healthy competitors to those in place already.

Still, although I would not dispute the reality of a sociological dimension of science, I do not believe that an exclusively sociological explanation of science can fully account for its empirical success. For example, how do we explain the unparalleled predictive success and explanatory power of scientific theories if the laws and theoretical terms of science are not in some way grounded in nature? In addition, I would surely take the data of science to be transcultural, reflecting something absolutely critical about the way the world really is, and without which we would have no hope of producing more humane technology.

Moreover, I fear that if we regard science as a purely cultural product, we will find it even harder to claim that other forms of knowledge could be free of a crippling relativity. If that were the case we would have left ourselves little ground for claiming anything normative or transcultural about the gospel, and we would thereby undercut our apologetic and prophetic stance. For how are we to avoid nihilistic relativism and speak out prophetically today if the moral authority of Scripture is totally circumscribed by its specific historical roots? How can the church stand over and against culture if it is in essence only the product of culture? Indeed it was through the transcultural power of the gospel, almost two thousand years ago in a town not far from where we sit today, that Paul overcame the illusions of the magician Elymas and converted the proconsul (Acts 13:4-12).

Moreover, the cost of relativizing science is that most scientists will reject that approach—and us as well. As you know, it is always extremely hard to get scientists, and the general public whom we want to influence, to take the concerns of the church seriously or to include church spokespersons in public debates. I fear that many scientists (who admittedly are "naive realists" about science and keep science and values rigidly separated) would react to an ideological critique by rejecting it out of hand. Hence we must be careful lest we undercut our prophetic stance and preach only to the "converted."

We must also recognize that, for its part, much of the church would move in the opposite direction, back into a rigid two-worlds dichotomy, opting for "spirituality" over against "praxis."

Finally, it seems to me that the sociological critique ends in its own denial, for it cannot ultimately survive its own critique. Thus for my part I would want to sharply limit the ideological critique to situations in which people hold destructive beliefs for social or political reasons but support them with seemingly scientific reasons (such as maintaining racist views for political reasons but supporting them with allegedly scientific arguments). Beyond this, the social dimension of religious or scientific epistemology seems to me to be a real, but in fact positive, factor that we can welcome.

We are therefore at a crossroads, and I simply lay it out to us all. How are we to build the new vision of the global church in a scientific/technological age? Although I believe this vision will involve a four-way discussion between science, technology, theology, and ethics, the way ahead does not lie with those who "wave the flag of ideology." Instead our strategy must begin, as it always does for the church, with an understanding of our own history.

◆ A PERSONAL NOTE ◆

Finally, how can I respond to the new horizons we have been opening up at Cyprus? Much of my time is devoted to teaching seminary students in the Master of Divinity programs of nine Protestant and

Roman Catholic seminaries of the Graduate Theological Union in Berkeley, California. I also work with doctoral students in our graduate school in the area of systematic and philosophical theology. This gives me the privilege of having some impact on the ecclesiastical and academic religious communities of the future. I would like to explore new directions for my courses and research that would involve a broader, more integrative perspective on science, theology, technology, and ethics.

During this week I have been thinking about several concrete examples of this new direction, and I'd like to share one with you now.

The idea is to identify a specific technology that by its very nature embodies both theological implications and ethical issues. A striking example is the laser. On the theoretical side, one can't understand a laser without studying classical optics, electricity, magnetism, and thermodynamics. Yet, above all, the laser works on some of the key principles of quantum physics.

So there you have it: The laser is a concrete instantiation of two vastly different paradigms in physics, the classical and the quantum, and as such provides a remarkable framework for discussing philosophical questions about science. Moreover each of these paradigms is essential to the theological task at hand as we work on understanding afresh the doctrine of God and the meaning of creation and redemption. Finally, the laser produced coherent light, an inviting new metaphor for the constructive relation of theology and science.

The laser is also a key instrument in a vast array of new technologies, each bearing on society and raising profound ethical issues for our time. One need only think of such areas as communication, nuclear fusion, the compact disk, and the Strategic Defense Initiative to begin to appreciate how many diverse technologies depend on this one unique invention, and how vastly different are their ethical profiles! Surely the laser instantiates the ethical dilemma, the juxtaposition of good and evil, and the task of making the hard choices contemporary technology brings to us in both the First and Third Worlds.

Speaking also as the director of the Center for Theology and the Natural Sciences, I would like to explore ways in which our program of conferences, public forums, church workshops, publications, and so on, can incorporate the perspectives arising out of conferences such as this one. A particularly important direction is through our growing involvement with a number of denominations that are beginning to seek ways to bring the "two cultures" together. As we help plan and convene such conferences we will have an ideal opportunity to facilitate the process by which the church becomes actively engaged in issues of theology, science, technology, and values. We also support basic research in systematic and philosophical theology, and here too the concerns of Cyprus can be voiced and heard more directly.

I also want to work more closely with those in the scientific community who want to hear the gospel in a language they can accept, for I see this as part of my own ministry. I want to speak for a flock in exile, if you like. Many of the perspectives taken for granted at a conference like this seem like a foreign culture to scientists— one they do not understand, from which they feel alienated, and which they reject. Though many scientists would have wanted otherwise, and though some may even still attend church on Sundays, the church has become for them a foreign culture. And so I also feel called to my own ministry, to return to the desert of the lab, to walk with my friends on their own sacred ground and to search with them for ultimacy, meaning, and compassion.

♦ BRIDGING THE CENTURIES ♦

And so we stand at the twilight of our century and the dawn of the next. In a time of uncertainty we know one thing for sure: There will be new theological movements as radically different from our own time as neo-orthodoxy, existentialism, death of God, deconstruction, liberation, and all the rest are from the movements of the nineteenth century. There will be new challenges to peace and justice, new demands on our vision and commitment, new horizons for our ministry. Hence our only real option is to forge ahead or be forgotten.

We are called to follow Christ, to set our hand on the plowshare and not look back, to let the dead bury the dead. We must pick up our crosses and follow him who always empowers us as only God can, who goes before us as supreme example and with us as dearest friend. Martin Luther and John Calvin did it four hundred years ago. Karl Barth and Martin Luther King, Jr., did it in our midst. And so must we.

Although in many ways our age is collapsing, we can hope with confidence that the church will survive because of the promise Jesus made to those first disciples beside the Sea of Galilee. Our task is to ensure that, as it survives, it continues to make sense of what it believes, to communicate the gospel to our changing world, and to motivate others to follow Christ the Way.

There is a unique feature to our period of change, though. Unlike other generations for whom the intellectual world was decimated by political and social revolutions, we can foresee and anticipate much of the change coming upon us, because we see it as our own product, the product of science and technology.

If we survive our nuclear madness, there will be a future in which our children's children will live and breathe, play and pray.

We must save what we can for them and create anew the vision of faith through the resources of the gospel. The single most important piece of our mission is therefore that we continue to reach out to each other across the space of this global village, and that we look ahead and reach out as well through time towards the future.

·11·

Six
Bible Studies

Paulos Mar Gregorios

♦ MONDAY ♦

The following Bible study was based on Gen. 1:1-3; John 1:1-14; and Gen. 3:1-7.

Does scientific knowledge belong to the original light of the Logos that was in each human person? Or is it derived from the secondary experience of the knowledge of good and evil that came of eating the fruit of the tree in the middle of the garden? That is our question. What kind of a thing is this science?

Among the ancient church fathers there was a general view that reason, or in Greek *logos,* is what makes humans participate in the light that was in the Logos of God. That is what the image of God means for many people.

No doubt both life and light are from God's Logos. They cannot come from the serpent or from any other created being.

But then, God created light. The light was good. He gave that light to human beings with some restraint. Then a subsequent experience of humankind, a bold, audacious choice of humanity, brought us to where we are today. The original light combined with this bold, audacious choice of humanity. Well, the immediate result of that combination was a bit of confusion—fig leaf breech cloths Adam and Eve made themselves to cover up, rather unsuccessfully I suspect. Yahweh then gave them something better—skin garments. That is what we are wearing now, according to the ancient fathers.

I wonder if Adam killed the animals first to make those skin garments. But the Bible does not say so. Did Yahweh kill the animals?

I don't know. Anyway, where did the skin come from? Never mind. Don't ask too many questions. In any case, the garments of skin seem to have stuck. According to some of the best thinkers among our ancestors, we still carry around these garments of skin. Gregory of Nyssa, my favorite, says that our mortal body is our garment of skin.

The original body that God gave us was obviously not quite like this one. Evidently it was a fairly grand thing, not bound by the force of gravity and not subject to dissolution, corruption, decay, or death. It could ascend into the atmosphere, as we saw in the ascension of Jesus. It could go beyond the veil of vision, which is the definition the ancients gave of heaven.

They do not think, at least the intelligent fathers do not think, that heaven is some kind of ceiling above which there is another floor. They define heaven as the limit of our sense perception. Beyond that is heaven. It could be right here but beyond the limit of our perception. Beyond that veil of vision Jesus, the incarnate human person, has gone. His is the kind of body that can enter through closed doors and thick walls.

Something that interests me even more is that the fathers said the body is capable of *eukinesis*—easy movement, movement by will. I wish I had *eukinesis* right now. Taking these garments of skin from India to Cyprus was a big job. If I had the original body I could have gone back and forth easily.

The body could suddenly appear with the two disciples on the road to Emmaus. Just as suddenly it could appear somewhere else. It could manifest itself where it willed. Its biggest privilege was to hover around the throne of God as the angels do.

Here the fathers introduce into the Christian tradition a very controversial doctrine: the doctrine of double creation. The present state of creation is the consequence of a double act. The first act is the original creation in which there is no presence of evil, but in which there is the freedom the serpent used. In the second creation, we got our garment of skin. And we now experience the limitations of this garment of skin, particularly subordination to the force of gravity.

Scientists tell me that gravity is a different kind of force from the other three: electromagnetism, weak force, and strong force. Gravity belongs to the nature of the cosmic curvature.

Gravity, of course, has its astronomical meaning, but as far as we human beings are concerned gravity is a consequence of the second creation. And that means that humanity can never be understood without reference to both creations. The first was the primordial beginning when God said, "Let light be," the creation that culminated in the emergence of the human. And the second creation occurred after humanity had used its freedom to disobey God, and God provided it with a temporary constitution of its body and of its sense, which are not necessarily part of its ultimate nature.

Although the second creation is the reality that we now experience, it is not primordial or final. We are expelled from the original primordial garden, wanderers on the face of the earth with knowledge of good and evil, cut off from the Tree of Life by the cherubim and the flaming sword, subject to sin and death, dust finally returning to dust. That is the second creation. But that is not the primordial nature of the human person.

Scientific knowledge—knowledge through modern science—shares in the ambiguity of this double creation. It comes from the breath of life and the light of consciousness with which humanity was endowed in the first creation. But it also shares in the character of the garments of skin and the expulsion from the garden where the Tree of Life stands, guarded by the fiery angel and the flaming sword. Human knowledge becomes ambiguous; the original light is clouded by the darkness of ignorance. Humanity can still seek for the original light that gave birth to the light in human consciousness. Humanity knows the good, the light of life, but is barred from access to it by the darkness of evil in it.

A Christian theological approach to scientific knowledge fails where it takes no account of this ambiguity inherent in our consciousness itself. It is the consciousness of a fallen humanity. But the original light, which is always good, is still there, though hidden by the darkness of evil.

And here an Eastern Orthodox theologian has to say a few words about the fall itself. We do not see in the teaching of the apostles any doctrine of total depravity. Nor do we have an expression for what the Augustinian tradition calls "original sin." The nearest we come to it is the concept of *propatorikon hamartēma,* the "sin of our forefathers," but not original sin. Our origin, including original creation and human birth, is not in sin. So we cannot speak of original sin. The fall does not make us totally evil. It is God who has made us these coats of skin and put us here, after the fall. The light still shines in the darkness; darkness has not overcome or put out the divine light in us.

We are fallen creatures, fallen from the original beatitude of our God-given inheritance. But we have not fallen into the abyss. We have fallen into the earth that God created and that is good. But it is a cursed earth. "Cursed is the earth because of you," God says to Adam. "In toil you shall eat of it all the days of your life" (Genesis 3). The fall does not take away life and light. It only makes them ambiguous, unstable, unreliable, distorted, obscured, unenduring. We are fallen from the garden of eternal delight, but we are not fallen out of the hands of God. We are deformed but not totally depraved. No one is righteous, but no one is totally evil either.

We go wrong if we think of science as simply belonging to the fallen world and, therefore, as evil in itself. Science too is ambiguous, not evil. Let us not forget the fact that modern science is born in a fallen *and* redeemed world. It partakes not only in our fallen-ness but also in our redemption in Christ. It is not without significance that science was born in a Christian milieu.

I am not interested in proving *The Religious Origins of Modern Science* with Eugene M. Klaaren and *The Origins of Science and the Science of Its Origin* with Father Stanley L. Jaki. What I am saying is that modern science arose in a world redeemed by our Lord Jesus Christ. It arose in a Christian Europe, but that does not make it any more Christian than would be the case if it had been born in Africa or Asia.

Modern science has its roots in the original light with which humanity is endowed. That light is distorted by sin, but it is also redeemed by the incarnation of Jesus Christ. That would be a theological understanding of the nature of science.

Modern science, however, is incapable of answering some of the very important questions raised by science itself. I have identified four clusters of such questions raised by science for which the answers have to be sought outside of science. Here is a brief outline of them:

1. Ethical issues produced by scientific developments
    a. Diagnosis by amniocentesis of genetic defects in an embryo in the womb. What action should follow?
    b. Peaceful use of nuclear energy. How much risk is justified after Windscale, Three Mile Island, and Chernobyl?
    c. Genetic engineering. What are the ethical norms to regulate it?
2. Science and socio-economic questions
    a. Who controls scientific-technological development and directs it to benefit a minority at the expense of the majority of humanity?
    b. Science/technology for war and profit to be liberated for service of the poor.
    c. Research and development concentrated in the developed countries.
3. Science and approach to reality
    a. If science is only one possible approach to reality, what is its relation to such other approaches as art, music, literature, religion?
    b. What are the roles of reason and faith in science, and in theology? How can they be reconciled, or integrated, or held in tension?
    c. What signs are there in science that point to the transcendent? What kind of truth does science reveal?

4. Science/technology and the shaping of humanity
   a. How does a scientific-technological and urban-industrial society shape human persons, societies, and institutional patterns of human existence?
   b. Does scientific training shape the human mind in a particular pattern of seeing reality which shuts out other aspects of reality? Is there distortion in scientific perception? In the attitudes of scientists and technologists towards other people?

These are some of the areas we need to keep in mind as we proceed.

♦ TUESDAY ♦

The following Bible study was based on Heb. 11:13; and Rom. 1:18-22, 28-31.

Faith (or *pistis,* basic trust) seems to be an essential element in both scientific understanding and religious understanding. In scientific understanding, however, the element of faith is often difficult to recognize.

Michael Polanyi points out two examples: (1) a fundamental faith in the effectiveness of the scientific method itself as a sure way to dependable knowledge, and (2) a trust in the work of previous scientists that the scientist accepts without empirically testing. Science itself cannot establish the scientific method by strict empirical proof according to its own criteria. This is the well-known definition or limitation of science.

The modern scientific enterprise is a community tradition based to a large extent on faith. By faith I mean trust in certain basic realities as dependable and reliable. This trust may be inspired by experience and by a particular interpretation of that experience. But it is not by any means dictated by unquestionable objective experience.

Here we must recognize the twin conclusions to which modern philosophers of science have come: Scientific affirmations or hypotheses are not without subjectivity, and they cannot be logically demonstrated or proved to be unqualifiably true. Objectivity and proof—the twin pillars on which science and scientism rested in the past—have effectively collapsed.

It is now recognized as irrefutable that all scientific theories are subjective-objective constructions of the human mind. Both in the construction of the theory itself and in the interpretation of the experimental results, an element of subjectivity is inescapable. No scientific theory is generated by experiments themselves. Theories are by definition subjective creations. They are tested by experiment and confirmed or discredited by experiment. Logically, however, the inductive method rests on the unprovable assumptions (1) that if in one thousand cases B always follows A, then B is caused by A, and (2) that in the case following the thousandth, B will follow A.

Operationally we can use such a hypothesis with a major degree of success. But that does not mean that the hypothesis is logically proved. It is only an assumption that reality is consistent and rule-governed, that our expectations of reality based on experience will be confirmed by the future behavior of that reality. But that kind of faith is absolutely necessary for the advancement of science. Without that basic faith, the whole edifice of science would collapse.

We know from experience that false theories can still be confirmed by experience. The typical case is the fact that for centuries people accepted the Ptolemaic or geo-centric view of the universe because much of the data seemed to confirm it. As Thomas Kuhn has made clear, at certain points the cumulative tradition of science undergoes paradigmatic revolutions, the Copernican revolution and quantum physics being paradigm cases of such scientific revolutions. Generally cumulative and occasionally revolutionary, the scientific enterprise has grown up as a continuing tradition within a specific community of scientists with a credo that changes from epoch to epoch. The credo of the eighteenth century or nineteenth century would be different from the contemporary credo.

I am not a scientist, but I will give you my version of a contemporary scientist's credo. Scientists know better than I what they believe, but as an outsider to the community of science I will try to communicate how the credo of the scientific community comes through to me.

A Scientific Community's Credo

"In the beginning was the Big Bang. The Bang was self-generating, and it is no use asking about the cause of the Bang or what it is that banged. The Bang was in the beginning. All things, including time, space, and causality were made by the Bang, and without the Bang nothing that ever was or is today could come to be.

"In the Bang was life, including the life and consciousness of humans. In the beginning the Bang was chaotic and formless, particles careening about in time-space created by the whirl that followed the Bang. At that stage there was no Newton or Newtonian mechanics. Everything jumped quantum leaps to growing stages of excitement. Finally the whirl condensed into plasma and gas, liquids and solids, stellar systems and planetary systems.

"Then came geo-physics, the formation of the oceans, the continents, the atmosphere and ozone layers, the ionospheres and continental drifts. The universe had warmed up and Carnot's Second Law of Thermodynamics began to operate. The things that had been warmed began giving off energy and moving from the wound-up state to one of dissolution or entropy, leading to the perfect equilibrium of death or zero entropy.

"Meanwhile another law had come into operation. The principle of that law, as well as the opposite law of thermodynamics, had been inherent already in the Big Bang. This was the law of life, which begins with the emergence of a self-replicating cell, a highly asymmetric protein molecule capable of growing to higher and higher degrees of complexity and centralized organization. This was negative entropy, the movement from a disorganized state to more and more organization. But finally entropy wins over negative entropy as organisms go into dissolution and die. The universe itself must die, because death is finally lord and king, until the next Big Bang comes."

I notice that the scientific community never uses the expression, "I believe." It seems to have difficulty acknowledging the place of belief within the scientific enterprise. But scientific assertions sound to me like statements of belief, interpretations of experience, convictions held in the community of science. That was the impression I got when reading Steven Weinberg's *The First Three Minutes.* I found no acknowledgment that the framework was largely a matter of belief—belief related to experimental facts, but still belief.

I am not ready to stand with Barbara Ward in making the claim that Christian theology is also a theoretical hypothesis that can be put to the test. She gave us a hypothetical formula for producing a Christian saint and challenged us to try it as a life-experiment and check if the predicted result, the formation of a Christian saint, would not follow.

I am arguing, instead, that the scientific enterprise is also a community tradition based on certain fundamental beliefs.

According to the author of the Epistle to the Hebrews, it is by faith that we understand certain things. For example, if there was a Big Bang at the beginning, the foundation of that Bang was in the word and will of God.

I prefer to see the creation in images other than the Big Bang. In the Christian community we believe that the big splurge of energy was an act of the Triune God, Father, Son, and Holy Spirit. In the Eastern Orthodox tradition we say that it was an idea-will-word act. By this we mean that in the creative act of God, the conception of that which is to be created, the will that it should come into existence, and the word-act by which the creation comes into being occur in the same instant. In human acts there is an interval between conceiving something, willing it, and finally producing the effect. In the divine act there is no such interval. And therefore we will not say with Steven Weinberg that the first millionth of a second in the Big

Bang cannot be explained but that everything that followed can be explained by science.

Instead we would say, along with the author of Hebrews (and not with Plato, who some people think is behind Hebrews), that the *blepomenon,* the visible reality or reality open to our senses, is only a dimension of a larger unmanifest reality. We do not believe that the *blepomenon* or *phainomenon* can be understood in itself without reference to the unmanifest *mē-phainomenon* on which it is contingent and dependent. The faith of the scientific community, based on its hope, is that the phenomenal universe is a self-contained and self-sustaining entity that can be understood in itself. This seems to me a faith for which there is no real ground. I would beseech Christian scientists to look at this faith, which seems to me a false faith and not at all necessary for the scientific enterprise. I wonder whether some competent Christian scientists would have the courage, knowledge, and wisdom to produce a paradigm that is less childish than that of the creationist school in North America. I ask, in ignorance, whether there is more than fear of ostracism from the scientific community that prevents Christian scientists from developing a paradigm of reality that takes into account our best real insights gained in the scientific enterprise.

The Moral Factor in These Assumptions

If the first chapter of Romans tells us anything, it is that humanity has enough evidence to acknowledge God, and if it ignores that evidence it is responsible for the moral consequences that follow.

The chapter also tells us that as a result of ignoring God, the heart *(kardia),* the center of the human personality, was darkened *(eskotisthē)* and has become unable to understand *(asunetos).* It is this moral clouding that breaks forth, not only in the personal and social sins that St. Paul has catalogued for us from the practices of the pagan society of his time, but also in the more frightening sins of war, nuclear peril, famine, exploitation, torture, misinformation, oppression, deforestation, and the upsetting of the eco-balance that sustains life.

We seem to be more sophisticated than ancient pagans. They knew God and yet ignored him, failing to give thanks (Romans 1:21). "Claiming to be wise, they became fools. They exchanged the glory of eternal God for images and idols shaped as mortal man or birds or animals or reptiles" (1:23). Our images and idols are not of animals and reptiles, but of a self-existent Big Bang to which we do not have to give thanks and which we do not have to worship. We just go on banging everybody else, in imitation of our scientific god, banging nature, banging other people, and banging ourselves in the process.

I need not say more. You are intelligent persons. You can see what all of this means. The only thing I want to say is that we are *anapologetos,* without an apology, without an excuse. We are responsible.

◆ WEDNESDAY ◆

The following Bible study was based on Heb. 2:5-18.

These meditations are intended to provide an orientation to a Christian approach to the world, and to the science/technology that deals with the world.

I say world. I do not say nature. Nature in the sense of all that exists, whether inclusive or exclusive of humanity, is a pagan concept. It is not a biblical category. The Old Testament does not use the category of nature. Only in 2 Maccabees, the apocryphal book originating in a Hellenized milieu, is the word nature (*phusis* in the Greek Septuagint) used in this sense. And there it is a pagan, Antiochus Epiphanes, who in trying to force the Jewish high priest to eat pork, says to him that it is a delicious food provided by "nature." In the New Testament the word *phusis* is used to denote the God-given character of an entity, such as human nature. The New Testament does not speak of the world as nature.

Nature, as a pagan category, denotes that which exists by itself as opposed to culture, which is made by human beings.

Christians should beware of falling into the temptation of speaking about "God, man, and nature" or "dominion over nature." We should speak of the world, or of the created order, not of nature, as if it were a self-existent reality independent of humanity and God.

God, Humanity, and the World

These three realities are known in three different ways. The way we know God, humanity, and world are methodologically distinct. In knowing the world, subject-object thinking may be justified and perhaps inescapable. But we cannot use that kind of thinking in relation to our selves, or to other human selves, or to God. Even in knowing the world we cannot be exclusively objective, but have to use subjective-objective thinking and understanding.

Modern science was born in a milieu in which the three entities—God, humanity, and world—were held together. But its later development has been in a framework that recognizes only two realities—the knowing subject and the known object. Descartes and Laplace laid the foundations for this dualistic thinking. Descartes spoke of *res cogitans,* the "thinking thing," as subject and *res extensa,* the extended or space-time world, as object. Laplace dispensed with God as an unnecessary hypothesis for understanding reality through science. Our whole modern culture is pervaded by this dualism of humanity as subject and "nature" or "external world" as object.

While modern science may have had its origin in a Christian framework, and in the Christian concept of a God-given and God-controlled, law-governed universe, the development of science has been spurred by the setting aside of Christianity's fundamental belief that both humanity and the world exist only in contingent dependence on God. If we overlook this fact, as many Christian historians of science do, we are likely to get into mistaken assessments of the scientific enterprise. This "secular" dualistic development of science is historically understandable, but we cannot afford to overlook its consequences out of some feigned respect for the scientific enterprise as such. This tendency to idolize science and stand in such awe of it as to prevent us from recognizing its true nature is, for a Christian, nothing short of blasphemy and idolatry. Until we recognize the idolatrous aspects of our attitude towards modern science, Christians cannot come to terms with it.

I know that what I have said is not acceptable to many of you in that form. I hope you can agree a little more if I say that "Christendom" is responsible for this secular dualistic development of science.

By Christendom, I mean essentially more than just the medieval church, which opposed the free development of science and against which the eighteenth-century Enlightenment had to revolt. I mean primarily the concept of *Christianitas* as developed by Charlemagne and his theologians as equivalent to the kingdom of God. As I read the writings of Charlemagne's theologians he tries to say that Christendom or *Christianitas* is the concrete manifestation of the kingdom of God on earth. That is what he wanted his Holy Roman Empire to be: the concrete manifestation of that city of God about which Augustine had written. These theologians had also the audacity to further falsify the truth by extending the equation to say: *Civitas dei* equals *Christianitas* equals *Romanitas.* The Holy Roman Empire of the non-Roman Franks was an expression of this false concept of a Christian world, a Christian empire, which was also a *renatio,* or rebirth, of the Christian Roman Empire of the fourth century, which had fallen to the Vandals.

It was this revised Christian Roman Empire of Charlemagne's Christendom that was identified with the kingdom of God on earth. It was the job of this Christendom not only to enforce God's will in the Holy Roman Empire, but also to expand it to the ends of the earth. The theologians and the clergy had the responsibility of interpreting the will of God from Scripture and tradition. The Holy

Roman emperor or his state would then translate that will into civil laws and enforce obedience to them.

The importance of this development of *Christianitas* for us here is its close association with *dominium terrae,* the domination of the earth. The interpretation of the Hebrews passage we have read refers primarily to the domination of the whole earth and bringing it into submission to the will of God. In the Christendom of Charlemagne, however, the emphasis was not on dominating the earth through science and technology but on a state-centered domination, a political economy controlled by the clergy and the feudal barons, theoretically expanding territorially to cover the whole earth and bringing it into obedience to the will of God by conversion or forced obedience. Charlemagne's Christendom developed only the idea of a Christian state-and-clergy controlled *dominium terrae,* stretching to the ends of the earth.

Charlemagne's Christendom remained a puny little affair in a corner of western Europe. It could not spread even to cover Spain or Italy or Britain or most of the Scandinavian countries, not to mention the Byzantine Empire, the rival Christendom flourishing to the East. Neither could it expand to the Islamic Caliphate of *Ispahan* (Spain). This little Christendom lacked the power to bring the two rivals, Eastern or Byzantine Christianity and Southern Islamic Spain, into submission. But it developed the desire to do so, along with the Christian justification for so expanding, and the hostility towards Eastern Christianity and Islam that came to clearer expression in the Crusades.

We cannot here deal even cursorily with the historical development of the idea of Christendom, which was identified with *Romanitas* and was later taken over by the Bishop of Rome as king of the kings and bishop of the earth, as the direct representative of Christ on earth. He took over the responsibility of enforcing the *dominium terrae* not only in Europe but also over the whole earth through the kings of Portugal and Spain. The Caliphate of Ispahan foolishly declared its independence from the Caliphate of the Abbasids and became a victim of Christian Europe. Christian Portugal and Christian Spain received the commission from the Pope to bring the whole earth under obedience to the will of God, obedience to Christ and to his vicar on earth, the Roman pope.

Africa, Asia, Latin America, and North America, which had existed as human societies for thousands of years, were suddenly "discovered." Trade, plunder, and slavery were now possible as ways of *dominium terrae.* Christendom expanded through trade, piracy, and colonial conquest.

It is in that ground that modern science has its roots. Historians of science usually ignore the double spur that early European science received from the needs of expanding the trade routes and the process of colonization, and from the material resources plundered or acquired by trade from the rest of the world. The *dominium terrae* concept was originally understood in terms of political economy, and only later in terms of science and technology. It did not develop in a Christian Europe isolated from the rest of the world, but in a Christian Europe in constant interaction with the rest of the world. It was spurred by that interaction into developing modern science and technology.

Tomorrow we must look at the more positive aspects of science and technology in the functioning of humanity between the two poles of God and the world. But today I want only to warn Christians against any idolatry of science that replaces the idolatry of "nature." Such idolatry will inhibit us from a free and honest assessment of science/technology as a gift from God.

♦ THURSDAY ♦

The following Bible study was based on Psalm 144.

Our Bible meditation continues on the theme "God, Humanity, and the World." We focus again on the question, What is humanity? What is man/woman? This question is raised in those terms at least four times in the Bible.

The first to have raised it seems to have been Job. So let me translate a passage from Job 7.

"Has not man a hard service upon earth? Are not his days like the days of a slave? My flesh is clothed with worms and dirt. My skin is hardened and breaks out afresh. Remember that my life is a breath, but I will not restrain my mouth. I will speak in the anguish of my spirit. I will complain in the bitterness of my soul.

"Am I the sea, or a sea monster, that you set a guard over me? When I say my bed will comfort me, my couch will ease my complaints, then you scare me with dreams and terrify me with visions. So much so that I would rather be strangled to death. I loathe my life. I don't want to live. Let me alone for my days are a breath. What is man that you make so much of him? And you set your mind on him. You visit him every morning. You test him every moment."

Those questions raised by Job have been raised in Hebrews 2:6-8 and by the psalmist in two other contexts. If we take these different contexts in which the question, What is humanity? has been asked, we get some interesting contrasts.

In Job it is a cry of anguish: "Why do I have to suffer this kind of life, why do I have to be afflicted like this, why can't I be left alone?" This is the complaint to God. Despair, but despair combined with trust.

That is one way of asking the question, What is humanity? Why do you make people suffer so much? Why do we have to go through Hiroshima and Nagasaki? Why do we have to go through concentration camps and holocausts? Why do we have to go through Vietnams? Why do we have to go through the 1947 riots in India and Pakistan, which killed hundreds of thousands of people?

It is a good question to ask along with Job. Sixty percent of the world's people still do not have enough to eat, or a place to sleep, or enough clothing. Why? What is humanity? That is one context in which we can ask that question.

The second context, from Psalm 8, is different. There you have, "Oh Lord, our Lord, how majestic is thy name in all the earth! Thou whose glory above the heavens is chanted by the mouth of babes and infants. When I look at thy heavens, the work of thy fingers, the moon and the stars which thou hast set up, what is man that thou art mindful of him and the son of man that thou carest for him?"

It is in contrast to the glory of God that you ask the question, What is humanity?

Then the psalmist goes on to say, "Yet, thou hast made him a little less than God and dost crown him with glory and honor. Thou hast given him dominion over the work of thy hand. Thou hast put all things under his feet; all sheep and oxen and also the beasts of the field, the birds of the air, the fish of the sea, whatever passes along the paths of the sea. Oh Lord, our Lord, how majestic is thy name in all the earth!"

That is an interesting context. On the one hand, there is this great, majestic, glorious God. In comparison, what is humanity? On the other hand, compared to the rest of creation, everything has been put under humanity. So humankind is crowned with glory and honor. It is a dialectic approach in Psalm 8.

In Psalm 144 we find another kind of contrast. Here God is a rock, a fortress, a stronghold; and here humans are just a breath, a passing shadow. Our impermanence is compared with the dependability and reliability of God. And in that context the question arises again, what is man that thou art mindful of him?

The fourth context is in Hebrews 2:5-8, which repeats the Psalm 8 contrast but puts a new twist on it. In Psalm 8 you have the glory of God compared to which man is nothing and the world compared to which man is pretty high, crowned with glory and honor. The same thing is in Hebrews, but with a new turn. Everything is not yet subjected to man. That everything should be subjected to him is his vocation. But what you see is Jesus, the only man to whom everything has been subjected. The people who are to share in Jesus have not yet got there. So the *dominium terrae* remains a vocation yet to be achieved. In fact, humanity itself remains a vocation to be achieved.

Here are four passages in which the Old Testament and the New Testament have asked this question, What is humanity? in the same words more or less. It must have been a frequent question in these cultures.

There is, however, another passage that has taken the central place in the Augustinian doctrine of man. It is in Psalm 51:5. "Behold, I was brought forth in iniquity and in sin did my mother conceive me." That was the central text for Augustine to understand man. He made a dreadful exegesis of it. "In sin did my mother conceive me" meant to him that the act of conception is a sin. Augustine said that without *concupiscentia* nobody can be born. That no human being can be born without lust was Augustine's affirmation. He believed that this lust, which leads to conception, is somehow that which determines human nature. Thus humans are sinful because they are born out of an act of *concupiscentia*.

Actually Augustine said that only in a sermon. He didn't make it so central. But other people later made it central, and made a mess of it. If you take Psalm 51:5 literally ("Behold, I was brought forth in iniquity") even giving birth is a sin. The mother is sinning. Unfortunately this passage in Psalm 51 became decisive for Western Christian anthropology.

We must come back to those four passages with which we have been confronted and try to find a way of understanding what humanity is.

Perhaps the best thing for me to do now is to refer to three concepts developed in the ancient Christian tradition apart from Augustine.

One is that humanity is a microcosm. What is implied is that everything that is in the cosmos is already in the human person. A prevailing pagan idea was that man is made of the same elements as the earth and the cosmos. Therefore, in man the cosmos is embodied.

My favorite father, Gregory of Nyssa, didn't like this microcosmos idea. He fought one half of it by bringing a very eloquent image. He said, "You say man contains all of the elements of the earth. Wonderful. But so does a cockroach. So, is a cockroach a microcosm also?

"You go wrong," he said, "in too easily going into the idea of microcosmos. That is not what defines humanity. But there is another way in which man is a microcosmos, and that we should take seriously. The same creative *energeia* of God that created matter and worked in that matter to bring forth plant life and then animal life also finally brought forth human beings." A very minor idea of evolution in an unscientific early form is already in Nyssa.

Nyssa takes the definitions of matter from Plato and Aristotle and the Stoics and refutes each of them. Then he asks, "What then is matter?" His answer is that matter is *energeia theou.* It is the energy of God—a very powerful modern idea.

If Gregory of Nyssa were a Platonist he would say that matter is formless, useless, void, meaningless, non-being. But that is not what he said. He said that matter is the energy of God—the energy of God in motion, in dynamic development that culminated finally in plant life, animal life, and human life.

Then he goes on to say something that is again fascinating. He said that the human being embodies not just all the elements of the dust but the three previous stages through which humankind has come. A human being is a microcosm in the sense of embodying the material, the vegetable, and the animal kingdoms within him or herself.

But that still is not Gregory's final definition. His definition springs from the vocation that man has received through being created after the image of God. You are not yet the image of God, he said. Only Jesus is the image of God. But that is the direction in which you must develop as the image of God.

He refuted the idea that the image of God is in the intellect or in reason. This very common Western idea is in Augustine himself. The idea is that intellectual reason, which separates us from the animals, makes us in the image of God. That is not Gregory's idea. He says the image of God is in both the soul and the body of the human, and he goes into a beautiful chapter about where the mind is located in the body. He says that the mind is located in the whole body of a person, a very modern idea. The brain, he says, has a certain specialized function of sorting out information, but information gathering is done by all parts of the body. And the body itself knows. It is not just the head that knows.

He has the idea that the creation of humanity did not consist of creating the soul first and then putting it into a body. The body and soul were born together and grow together. For him, therefore, the image of God does not mean just the invisible. He will not accept the argument that because God is invisible, that which is invisible in us, the mind, must be the image of God. He says something that at first shocks. He says the body is also made in the image of God. That sounds like anthropomorphism, as if God has hands and legs and feet and eyes. That is not what he means.

He says: Look at humans. What is the most distinctive thing about them? How are they different from the animals? The difference is not just in the head, because animals also have brains. But the animal has to carry its body in a horizontal position. And the four feet support this body and the head, which is always bowing towards the earth.

Gregory says once human beings were able to stand on two feet, all kinds of changes took place. No longer were the arms used to support the body, but they are in the service of the brain. And the hand and the brain together know.

It is a modern concept again. The hand and the brain together know things, not just the brain alone. In modern thinking, as you know, theory and praxis are dialectically related to each other. It is out of the handling of material stuff that a human being grows up to be a human being.

Gregory says that once the head is lifted up the person doesn't have constantly to use his nose to look for food. Once his hands are free his tongue is free from the need to pick up food. He can develop language. And by this combination of brain, language, and hands a human being becomes the image of God. So in the body itself the image of God is reflected.

But what then is the image of God? Is it the body? No. Gregory defines the image of God in a very simple way, a definition that has been regarded as semi-Pelagian in the West but that I find most acceptable. He says God is good; therefore, the character of the image is to be good. The image of God is to be good like God. Good means to have power, wisdom, and love. And when these things are embodied and made real in this humanity, then humanity comes into the image of God.

I want to say at this point that this business of the use of the hand and the handling of matter is an essential aspect of growing into the image of God. So it is significant that using the brain and handling matter are what science and technology mean to people. Separating science and technology does not work because there is no modern technology without modern science, and modern science cannot do research without technology. You take something, understand how it works, and then make it work according to human purposes. That is science and technology. Science tells you how things work. Once you know that, technology can tell us how to work on things so that they work for us. Understanding how things, plants, animals, planets, whatever they are, work is science. And then you use that knowledge to make them work according to your human purposes. That is technology.

So this *stoff-wechsel*, this handling of matter, this metabolism and transforming of matter, this humanization of nature, is the process by which we become human beings. That is a very subtle concept. It is not simply that we become an image of God but it is the process of *menschwurden*, the process that Hegel talked about, by which one becomes a human being. I understand that that word in German is the same word as "incarnation" or "man becoming." Humankind is becoming through the *stoff-wechsel* or metabolism or material exchange of science/technology. So science/technology plays a major role in shaping the image of God in humankind. That is why you can't put it outside the concern of religion. You can't say that it is somebody else's business to look after science while we look after souls. Science/technology is a part of the means by which *menschwurdung*, becoming a human being, takes place. Therefore we must have a positive understanding of science/technology.

In spite of my warning against the idolatry of science and technology, I want to say that science and technology have a central significance in human becoming. Incarnation is human becoming. Incarnation is God in humanity becoming humanity. And in that process there is a central role for science and technology. So when I speak about *theosis* or deification, I have in mind that we take this whole nature, which has been given to us, and let the whole of it bear the name of God. "Nature" or world-with-humanity becomes a manifestation of the good. It becomes a manifestation of love, power, and wisdom. That is why science and technology are central to a Christian anthropology, to the understanding of human deification.

Deification is not that we human beings somehow become exactly like God. It is that we who embody the whole creation and are the priests of creation take the created order and shape it to show forth the glory of God. That is the vocation of humanity.

I shall continue this discussion tomorrow when I speak about humanity as the frontier being.

◆ FRIDAY ◆

The following Bible study was based on Gal. 4:1-7, Gal. 4:31-51, and 1 Peter 5:8-9.

Galatians 4:1-7: "I say, therefore, as long as the heir of a family is a child there is no virtual difference between him and his slave. The heir is, of course, lord of all, owner of all, yet he is put under tutelage of guardians and trustees until the time set for him by the father. The same is true of us as human beings. As long as we are children we are governed, enslaved by the elements of the world. But when the fullness of time comes, when maturity arrives, God sends his Son, born of a woman. Born subject to the limitations of law in order that he might buy out those who were under the law so that we may receive full adoption as children. And because we are now mature children of God, God has also sent forth the Spirit of his Son into the deepest recesses of our personal and social existence. So we cry out, *Abba*, Daddy, Father, because we are no longer slaves, but children. And if children, then we are heirs of God."

Galatians 4:31-51: "So, brothers and sisters, we are not children to be guarded by nurses, but we are children of freedom, children of the free woman. It is for this freedom that Christ has freed us. Therefore, stand fast in that freedom. Do not let yourselves be put again under the yoke of slavery."

1 Peter 5:8-9: "Be alert, watchful. Our enemy is prowling around like a hungry lion seeking prey to devour. Stand up to him, strengthened by faith. Do not be put down by your sufferings. Such suffering is the prescribed lot of the brotherhood throughout the world."

I want to speak about three aspects of the relation between God, humanity, and the world.

First, I want to talk about humanity as a frontier being. This is a central concept in patristics, humanity as a *methorios* being. *Methorios* does not mean frontier as the farthest limit. The frontier between two entities, the common area between the two, is the meaning of *methorios* as frontier.

The *methorios* participates in the reality on both sides of it. If you draw a line between two realities, it is a frontier. But that line participates in the realities on both sides. So what we mean by saying humanity is a frontier being is that humanity stands between the Creator and the creation as one who participates in both—in Creator and in creation.

Humankind is the breath of God. But humankind is also the dust of the earth. So it is not sufficient to have an inclusive view of nature in which you somehow put humanity inside nature. You must put humanity inside God too.

An inclusive view of God will be necessary if you take the frontier notion seriously. This view may be difficult because we have tried to turn the frontier into a gap between Creator and creation. But we who stand here in the gap are to be included, so to speak, in both. That is what is meant by our deification. It is participation in God. 2 Peter 1:4 clearly says we are called to participate in God's nature. That is what I mean by frontier being, this participation in both God and world.

The great temptation, on the one hand, is to forget God and become active in the world, solving the problems of the world by our activism. That is one temptation. When the activism doesn't work, however, we are tempted to go to the other end away from activism into contemplation, meditation, Eastern religions, all that. Our temptation is either to be simply activist in a secular world, trying to find fulfillment and solutions to problems through that, or to retreat, when that doesn't work, into a kind of internal world of contemplation and Eastern spirituality that is unrelated to the problems of society.

Neither extreme is permitted for us. We have to remain at the frontier between the two. It is our job to bring the creation to God, to speak to God in worship as the representative of creation, and, more difficult, to bring the person of God into creation so that the immanence of God is manifested through the human presence in the creation. A frontier being is one who lifts up the creation and speaks as the mouthpiece of creation in worship and one who brings the Creator inside the creation through his or her presence. This is the frontier existence of humanity.

There is another frontier in which the same choice is not given to one. That is the frontier between good and evil.

Any doctrine that assumes humans are intrinsically good or intrinsically evil will not do. Both must be recognized. Humankind is on the frontier, participating in both good and evil. But there its struggle is not to reconcile the two. It is to bring the good inside the evil, suffering and dying if necessary, but in that process redeeming that which is evil from evil.

That this frontier existence is part of our freedom is a point I want to clarify. Augustine speaks about *liberatas maior* and *libertas minor,* the major freedom and the minor freedom. The major freedom is the freedom to choose between good and evil. The minor freedom is the freedom to choose between different kinds of good. Minor freedom is within the good, choosing between different goods. And the other freedom, choosing between good and evil, is the *libertas maior.* In his prayers Augustine says, "I don't want this major freedom. Keep me within the minor freedom. Keep me inside the good so that I will have only this freedom. I don't want that big freedom."

The Eastern fathers would not accept that. They said you must face the first freedom all the time. You must stand on this frontier between good and evil. You cannot expect now to be freed from this struggle between good and evil to which you are called. It is in that context that your freedom will develop. To develop freedom you have to go right into the heart of that reality where the struggle between good and evil is going on, bringing about the victory of the good by suffering, by death, by love that gives of itself.

I want to say one more thing about humanity. (I'm glad it is now regarded as sexist to use the word *man* and that we are forced to use the word *humanity,* for the word *humanity* helps us to see that we are not talking about individuals. Humanity is one corporate reality.) Gregory of Nyssa, in an exegesis which is questionable, says that the one lost sheep for which the shepherd left the ninety-nine is not an individual sheep. All of humanity is a lost sheep. So the shepherd leaves the ninety-nine—the angels and everybody else there—and comes looking for the lost sheep, which is the whole of humanity. Of course, in the biblical context the exegesis is a bit difficult. But that is the freedom of patristic exegesis.

This interpretation has some implications that are worth noting. Our idea, and I heard it long ago from my good friend Billy Graham, is that the only way to solve the problems of the world is to make everybody Christian. He has changed his point of view since then. But when it was my privilege in 1953 to introduce him to a gathering at Princeton, that is what he said to me. You make everybody Christian and then everything will be all right. I told him that I find that people who are Christians also create many problems.

We have to come to a new understanding of the relation between the church and the whole of humanity. We cannot bring the whole of humanity into the church. History makes that very clear. Humanity must exist along with the church. The church must not be concerned only about its own salvation. It must constantly seek the salvation of the world by its presence in the world, by leavening the whole of humanity. Christ died for the whole of humanity and not for the church alone.

Recently it was my privilege to chair a conference on global issues in which one of the speakers was Ivan Frolov, the president of the Institute of Philosophy in the Soviet Union and an advisor of Gorbachev. He said one of the ideas now current among Russians is that they have become convinced that they cannot wait until everybody becomes Communist to solve the problems of the world. That is what Christians also ought to say. We cannot wait until everybody becomes Christian to solve the problems of the world.

They are saying that as a Communist party they must now live with other people who are not Communist and who are opposed to Communism and must work with them. Probably we have to say the same thing. We as Christians have to work with people who are not only not Christian but are opposed to Christianity. This includes Muslims, Buddhists, and Communists.

So when I talk about the freedom of humanity and the frontier beingness of humanity I am not talking only about the church. I am talking about the whole of humanity within which the church is an essential element, as its conscience, as its worshiping element. The church derives its significance by living with and for humanity as a whole.

My second point is about the nature of freedom. I don't want to go into all the foundational discussions about freedom from, freedom for. The freedom of God is both from and for. In one piece. Rather I want to say that freedom is freedom from internal and external constraints to create that which is good. Both this freedom from constraints and creation of the good are integral to freedom. One doesn't exist without the other. We have to be liberated from both internal and external constraints *in order to create the good*. And creating the good, not liberation from constraints, is probably the more important part of freedom.

Liberation Is a Means to Creative Freedom

The misunderstanding of freedom is that it is only liberation from constraint, so that one is free to do what one wants. Freedom has made you free, but do not use freedom as a platform for evil. Freedom is for doing good. Freedom is the creativity of the good.

Keeping those double aspects of freedom in mind will help you to understand when I say God is freedom. He is free from internal and external constraints, free to create that which is good. Good that does not come out of freedom, according to Gregory of Nyssa again, is not real good. The good of a beautiful flower is not the kind of good we have to produce. It is a good coming out of freedom. It is a good coming out of will. The connection of freedom to the will is very important. The will must be liberated from all bondage to external and internal constraints in order to will and do the good.

Now I want to say that freedom is built into the creation. When God brings the creation into being, it is already endowed with freedom. It is that freedom that we now begin to see at the most micro-level of matter and energy. Total predictability is not there. There seems to be an element of freedom in the behavior of the wave-particle, of the electron, of the minutest particles.

This same freedom grows and develops finally in human consciousness, which is probably the most sophisticated entity of which we have any awareness. (If you want to locate it in the brain, go ahead. The brain itself is the most highly evolved, complex organism that we know.) It is the same freedom that is in the micro-level that has in the grace of God broken out into human consciousness.

This continuity of freedom within the created order is becoming part of the new understanding of science. Even in biological evolution they say the evolutionary process made some important choices millions of years ago, such that if the choices had gone the other way, consciousness would not have emerged. That is what George Wald, biologist and Nobel Prize winner and once professor of biology at Harvard, tells me. He says the world has been built and guided in such a way that consciousness must emerge at the end. The choices that now permit the emergence of consciousness had already been made by evolution millions of years ago.

This element of freedom and consciousness that is present in the whole of creation comes to its full flower in humanity. It is humanity that is the consciousness of the creation. The creation responds to God through humanity and the creation has now the possibility of being guided by this consciousness, which has emerged in humankind as the brain of the cosmos.

This human consciousness, however, is in bondage to evil and has to be rescued from that bondage. Freedom has resulted in evil, by choice. Freedom grows by the struggle against evil. Creation has to be rescued from the bondage of that evil and be made free again to do what it was intended to do. That is what Christ has done. That is what the Spirit of Christ, which he has sent to us as we become mature, is enabling us to do.

Let me take the third problem, which is the problem of evil. Evil is pre-human but not pre-creation. The serpent was created and was in the garden before human beings got into trouble. So it is pre-human. Before humans fell into evil, evil had already existed in the creation. Evil comes out of the freedom of the created being.

Evil is not an impersonal force. If you say the Devil is only a force I can't accept it because this force is very cunning. And cunningness is not possible for a force. A force will have to be straightforward. The Devil is always deceitful, cunning, sly. You know how he can get inside us, inside the church. He has had much success because he has concentrated for some time on the church. As soon as we are no longer a threat to him, he leaves us alone. We are already caught. He is very sly, very intelligent. For the Christian to be alert, to be watchful, is very important, for this force constantly tries every trick to put us back into slavery.

I want to conclude by saying that Christ changes the spiral of evil in which we as humanity have been caught. Not only as Christians or as individuals but as humanity we were caught in a spiral of evil that could have led to our destruction long ago. Christ has reversed the spiral. We now have the possibility of using our freedom to go up in the spiral leading toward God.

But we must not go up alone. We must take the creation with us. The main job of freedom today is to take creation with us up the spiral of good, out from the spiral of evil. As we both offer it to God and accept the presence of God in creation it becomes a manifestation of God.

That is the meaning of the God, humanity, and world relationship—as I see it.

♦ SATURDAY ♦

The following Bible study was based on Col. 1:15-23.

I would like to sum up what the *dominium terrae* or the subjugation of the earth means. Since God put all things under the feet of humankind in Jesus Christ, we shall try to see the relationship between Jesus Christ, his body, and the world.

Let me read from Colossians 1:15-23. "He, Christ, is the icon of God, the manifest form of the unmanifest. First born of all creation, born before creation, since all things—those beyond the horizon of our senses as well as those on earth—were created in him. All things, including such institutional structures as kingships, lordships, regimes, and authorities, were created through him and for him. He himself is. He is prior to all things. All things hold together in Christ. He is the head of the body, the church. He is the originating principle, the first born from the dead as well. So he becomes the first in all things. It was in him that the fullness of being was pleased to dwell. And so to bring together all things to him he made peace by the blood of his cross, reconciling all things, those here on earth and those beyond in the heavenlies. And you also, formerly alienated from God, at enmity with God through works of evil, are now reconciled in the body of his flesh through death. And you are to be presented to God, holy, without blame or reproach before him. One condition is that you stand firm in the faith, steadfast, unwaveringly holding on to the hope of the gospel you have heard, the gospel proclaimed to all creation on this side of heaven. Of this gospel I, Paul, have become the humble servant."

The vocation of humanity to frontier existence was perfectly fulfilled by Jesus, the God-anointed Christ. He alone has fulfilled this mediatorial frontier function of the human person. He alone truly mediated God to the created order by his entering the created order as a created human being. He, the true breath of God, became the true human being of the earth, flesh of our flesh, dust of the earth like the rest of us, but also our captain, our elder brother, one of us, one with creation, partaking of matter and human flesh. So this double mediation of bringing God into creation and then taking creation back to God has been fulfilled in his life.

This is reflected most deeply in Philippians, in the great *kenosis* hymn: "Let this be your attitude, as it was that of Christ Jesus. He was born and subsisted as the form of God. But he did not cling to that status of being equal to God, but was willing to empty himself and took the form of a servant and became a human being. And finding himself as a human being he submitted himself further to the point of death and to the humiliating death on the cross."

So it is this Christ who emptied himself in order to become one of us who is now the priest of creation, who stands on behalf of the whole creation. The creation is, so to speak, the congregation for which he is the priest. Yet he is entirely one of us. Thus he becomes the true frontier being.

I want to emphasize that it is inside this created order— invaded by God, penetrated by God in Jesus Christ, and now being lifted up to God—that science and technology originate and grow.

Science and technology are not a natural outcome of the process of random evolution. Evolution is both physical and biological. But within that process there now is humanity capable of transforming it. It is extremely important that within the process of biological evolution humanity appears, capable of guiding it and probably also capable of destroying it. We must see this role of humanity in Jesus Christ as the captain of the physical, biological, evolutionary process. Science and technology, the most powerful tools ever given to humans, can be part of the redeeming process if they are themselves redeemed.

Science and technology also need to be redeemed and become servants of God's redeeming economy in Christ. Only a redeemed science/technology can serve the purposes of God both in biological evolution and in Christ, becoming part of that evolutionary process and guiding it up towards God.

This I believe is the true *dominium terrae*. Not simply controlling nature by science/technology but redeeming science/technology itself and guiding the ship of biological evolution towards its God-given purpose.

I want to say something about the church. The church is called the fullness of Christ. The church's function is constantly to be in dialogue with the whole of humanity and to remind humanity of its vocation to guide everything towards the good. Ephesians 1:22 says, "God has put all things under Christ's feet and has given him as head over the whole church, this whole church is his body, the fullness of him who fills and completes all things in every way."

The church has the fullness, has the *pleroma*. This *pleroma* is very significant and important for our understanding. Unfortunately we have lost touch with the intellectual milieu in which the concept arose. So I would like to talk to you about three meanings of *pleroma,* each of which is important for this discussion.

Pleroma in the ordinary sense means fullness. If you have a jar full of water, the water is the fullness or the content of the jar.

But it can also mean something else that is measured by physical fullness. I hope you know what an hour glass looks like. The top chamber is filled with fine sand and is used to measure time. Both the top and bottom chambers are marked so that you can know one o'clock, two o'clock, three o'clock. When the lower chamber fills to a certain point, that is the time appointed for the court to begin. In front of the courthouse will be a big hour glass in which the sand is constantly falling, and when it comes to a particular point you know that the court is assembled. That is the sense in which the New Testament uses the word fullness of time. God sent his Son in the fullness of time.

But there is a *pleroma tōn kairōn,* which is slightly different. Ephesians 1:10 speaks about the fullness of hours, or the decisive hour. That is not the hour of Christ's incarnation but the final hour when all things are put under Christ's feet. Both are fullness of time, the fullness of time for the incarnation and the fullness of time when all things shall be put under Christ's feet.

So we are between the two fullnesses of time. We are between the *pleroma tōn chronōn* in which the incarnation took place (Galatians 4:4) and the *pleroma tōn kairōn,* which is the final appointed hour when the fulfillment will take place.

There is another meaning of *pleroma* that was important in the milieu in which Colossians and Hebrews were written. It is a gnostic meaning. The Gnostics made a distinction between fullness of being, or *pleroma,* and shadow, which they developed into a fundamental tenet of their faith. They held that there is fullness of being, *pleroma,* and there is shadow being. The *pleroma* for the Gnostics was the place from which the savior comes to take us out of this shadow world and back into the fullness. That was the gnostic understanding of salvation. The word *savior* was an important term for them, and Christian Gnostics applied their understanding of the concept to Christ. So Christ came from the heaven for us, individual souls, to take us from this world of shadow back in the *ogdoad,* the fullness of being. Unfortunately, much of modern Christian fundamentalism works on this same understanding of salvation. The savior comes from above this world to pick up a few souls and goes back there so the souls can be with him.

It was in opposition to this kind of *pleroma skia* understanding that both Hebrews and Colossians were written. The epistle to the Colossians speaks of festivals, sabbaths, and new moons as *skia ton mellontōn,* a shadow copy of that which is to come. Colossians 2:17 speaks about this. The King James Version reads, ". . . which are a shadow of things to come, but the body is of Christ." The Revised Standard Version has fouled up the meaning by translating the passage as ". . . these are only a shadow of what is to come but the substance belongs to Christ." There is no justification whatsoever for translating *soma* as substance. *Soma Christou* cannot be translated as substance of Christ. To me the meaning is that the coming reality is the body of Christ.

That is a very bold statement. The coming reality is the body of Christ.

This is the context in which we come to the third meaning of *pleroma.* Ephesians 1:23 says the church is the body of him, the fullness of him who in everything fills all. This third meaning points to that which fills out and completes. We see the sense in Matthew 9:16, which says, "No one sews a patch of unshrunk new cloth onto an old garment for that which fills up the garment will tear away from the garment so that there is a worse tear in it." The word used for "that which fills up the garment" is *pleroma.* The patch that you sew on to fill a hole in a garment is called a *pleroma.* If you have a glass three-quarters full and if anybody asks you what is the *pleroma* of that glass, it is not the three-quarters of content but the one quarter necessary to fill it. That which will complete and make it full is the *pleroma.* This is the sense in which the church is the *pleroma.* The church fills out and completes the incarnate Christ.

The church also fills out and completes the sufferings of Christ, according to St. Paul. To understand how all things are to be subordinated to Christ and how humanity, the church, and the rest of the world are related to this process, we need a further theological understanding of who Christ is. And we need to do it in four dimensions, not space-time dimensions, but four dimensions.

First, there is Jesus Christ, the historical person. That is the initial dimension of the incarnate Christ. He was on earth for a limited period of thirty to thirty-five years and has gone beyond the visibility horizon and is at the right hand of God as our high priest.

The second dimension is Christ with his body, the church. Jesus Christ wanted to share the rule with his body, so the body is incorporated into him. By the body I mean more than just the Christians who are now living. I mean all the people whom Christ has drawn into his body from the beginning—the apostles, Mary, the prophets, the martyrs, all the Christians who have gone on before us, those of us who are here now, and those to come in the future. These together constitute the body, the fullness of him that fills all in all. That is the second dimension of Christ.

The third dimension is Christ with humanity. Christ did not assume only the church in the incarnation. He assumed humanity. Although the church is his body, Christ assumed the whole of humanity in its fullness. In some strange way that I cannot theologically formulate, Christ is related to all humanity in a very specific way. It is not exactly the same as his relation to the church where he is acknowledged, where he is constantly praised, worshiped, adored, loved. Even among those who do not acknowledge him the incarnation makes a profound difference because it is their humanity too that he has assumed. That is why we cannot dismiss other religions or the atheists or the unbelievers as if they have nothing to do with Christ.

Christ did not assume only one man, Jesus, but Jesus Christ assumed the whole of humanity. It is within that humanity that science and technology function. To ignore that aspect can be dangerous.

The fourth dimension is the eschatological dimension, the dimension of the final fulfillment. Ephesians calls it *anakephalaiosis,* the gathering up of everything under one head. This includes more than humanity. It includes all in heaven and earth, principalities and powers, angels, whatever existences there are, including material existences and organic life. All these are finally to be added up. That is the fourth or cosmic dimension of Christ.

Unless we keep all these four dimensions—the incarnate Jesus Christ who is our high priest, Christ with his body, Christ with humanity, and Christ with the whole cosmos in the eschatological final reconciliation—unless we keep all these four in their relation to each other, we will be misunderstanding the nature of Christ and will be trying to corner Christ for us as Christians. When somebody asked Gandhi, "Why aren't you a Christian?" he said, "I would have been a Christian but for the Christians." His experience with the Christians, especially in South Africa, was decisive for him. Let not Christians think that Christ belongs to us, as our property. We go and hit other people with Christ, as if he were our man. No. He is the one in whom they and we all exist.

This corporate entity called humanity is, like the church, a process. Those who have gone before, those who are coming behind are all one flow of humanity. This humanity does not exist in isolation from the rest of creation. Humanity cannot survive without the biosphere. And not only biosphere is essential. Everything in humanity seems to be dependent—on air and water and food, but also on the sun. And the sun itself is dependent on other systems. The corporate entity of humanity exists as part of so many systems. I read just last week of a flow, a solar wind coming from the sun and enveloping the earth in a kind of cushion. This flow travels at supersonic speed constantly from the sun. It is not visible to our eyes because it is plasma. We understand now that the space near earth is not a vacuum, but a plasma above the stratosphere. It is not empty. We are, so to speak, cradled by the sun, supplied by the energy of the sun. This earth and the sun are all of one package and this corporate humanity exists within that package; without that package, it cannot exist.

The relationship between humanity and the known created order is very complex. One of the processes of that relationship is humanization—changing nature, dealing with nature, exchanging with nature, and thus becoming human and making the planet human.

The humanization of creation on our planet has three dimensions. I shall mention them and then leave it there.

The first dimension is science and technology. Without this *stoffwechsel*, this constant interacting with nature, we could not get food or other necessities. Human existence is based on science and technology's dealing with nature.

The second dimension is the political economy, in which the social sciences also play a major role. Organized human labor, not just single individuals, deals with the world. And as soon as human labor becomes organized it becomes involved in a political economy. Political economy is dealing with nature and with each other in that process.

This is where I have to say something very strong: Let us not pretend that science can be isolated from the package of science/

technology or from the package of science/technology/political economy. If we try to isolate science we misunderstand it. Science does not exist in isolation, up in the air. It exists only as an enterprise of organized humanity within a political economy. It does not exist as an ideal reality.

The third dimension is culture with its value choices. It involves the activity by which we transform matter into expressions of beauty and truth, the expressions of a humanly created reality.

These three dimensions are all bound up together. Culture is closely linked to science/technology, which is closely linked to political economy.

It is in this kind of a world that the church as the body of Christ is asked to serve, to listen, to dialogue. "Brothers and sisters in the world, what have you found out ... tell us?" Then as we converse with them we also think with them about how to use what we have found out for the best purposes of the kingdom of God. That is the dialogue of faith and science—religious people finding out from the community of those who are actually doing the scientific/technological work what they have learned about how things work and how to work on things. In that process we identify ourselves with them and their dilemmas, not telling them the "truth" with authority. We cannot tell them which way science/technology should go. But when talking with them, we can ask, "Shouldn't it go this way rather than that way?"

A major part of research now deals with how to kill more people with less effort. And another major drive of research is how to get the most profit with the least investment. These have become two dominant purposes around which science and technology are largely oriented.

Redeeming science and technology is a job not just of the Christians. It must be done by the scientists and the technologists and the political economists and all of us together. True *dominium terrae* will come when we, along with our brothers and sisters in the other religions, along with the unbelievers, along with our brothers and sisters in the scientific community whether Christian or non-Christian, when all of us together struggle—struggle through suffering, struggle through pain, struggle through occasional conflict—to make sure that creation is going in the direction in which God wants.

International Roundtable

Verlyn L. Barker

One feature of the 1987 conference on "The New Scientific/Technological World: What Difference Does It Make for The Churches?" was an international roundtable. The roundtable consisted of church and educational leaders who were in strategic positions for integrating the findings and recommendations of the conference into a feasible program of work. Their objectives were: (1) to envision how the church may be engaged in issues of science and theology in the twenty-first century, (2) to assess the resources and work now in place, (3) to determine the structures that need to be created to implement the church's continued engagement, and (4) to plan immediate and specific next steps for the future.

♦ SUBSTANTIVE ISSUES FOR FUTURE PLANNING ♦

The roundtable identified a series of concerns that need to be addressed by the church in the future. It was understood that these concerns would be viewed within the context of the recommendations from the conference's regional groups.

Theoretical Issues: Questions of Epistemology, Methodology, Language

(1) Formulating a new natural theology, a theology of creation, with participation of persons from the different theological traditions and the multiple cultures in which theological formulation has distinctive marks, symbols, and images; and with the participation of scientists, unchurched Christians, and agnostics.

134

(2) Understanding and addressing the challenge of science to epistemology, methodology, and language, in search for a meaningful articulation of truth.

(3) Creating new theological symbols appropriate to the age of science and technology.

(4) Clarifying the role of biblical texts in light of modern and postmodern scientific world views.

Ethical Issues

Ethical issues arise for the scientist in decisions about the research in which he or she will be engaged, often stemming from the sources of funding for particular projects. Scientists also face the dilemma of their responsibility for an analysis of the possible uses of their work: Will it result in the welfare or abuse of humanity? What is the responsibility of the scientist in addressing the moral uses of his or her work?

The ethical issues raised by the uses of science and technology become the place of engagement where most people encounter the effects of science and technology, whether they be in regard to ecology, environment, nuclear energy and byproducts, medicine, or agriculture. These issues force ethical decisions about how much control people have over the use of technology, how they can safeguard its use for the enhancement of humanity.

Issues of the Impact on Social, Political, and Economic Structures of Society

In both the First World and the Third World there is an emerging consciousness about the pervasive impact of new science and technology on the total fabric of society and on furthering injustice. Examples are the use of nonrenewable natural resources, changes in patterns of family and community life, and ownership of technology by government and industry.

Issues of the Shaping of Humanity by Science and Technology

That science and technology are increasingly used in making social decisions raises questions about the appropriateness of seeking to direct scientific research and technology. The rather uncritical use of the computer in the schools, for example, raises questions about how that use will affect the development of critical thinking. Likewise, new medical technology creates tendencies to view the body as a machine rather than as a human organism.

Issues in the Internal Life of the Churches

There was consensus in the roundtable that the church faces a host of problems in getting prepared to take on issues raised by science and technology. Some of the issues are:

● pastoral care of scientists and technologists.

- effective preaching in an age of science and technology.
- meaningful liturgies that are mindful of contemporary world views.
- definitions of mission that make sense amidst contemporary realities, including the realities of science and technology.
- determining the appropriate role and function of the church in its educational work and in its participation in the formation of public policy amidst the discussions between science and theology.
- creating a process of continuing engagement so the church is prepared for new issues instead of being essentially reactive.
- creating networks so persons in a common inquiry may link in their quest and work.

◆ FACTORS FOR GUIDING FUTURE ENGAGEMENTS ◆

The roundtable identified factors that are pertinent to future engagements in theology and science.

1. The discussions should acknowledge the distinctive, but integrally related, nature of theoretical and ethical issues. They must not be separated lest the theoretical become only the intellectual exercise of a few and lest the ethical lose its theological foundations.

2. Persons from a variety of categories should be included in the discussions: experienced scientists and theologians, especially younger persons in both fields; persons from the First and Third Worlds; women and men; persons from the existing centers, institutes, and academies; and persons from new initiatives in various sectors of society, including industry.

3. The church structures must be challenged to define mission in light of contemporary realities, including the world view of science and technology. They must be asked to provide staff and budget for continuing attention to science and theology.

4. The church needs to face up to the need for new theological formulations that make sense to an age of science and technology, seeking formulations as relevant today as were the traditional formulations in the day in which they were written. The church needs to recognize that contemporary life is shaped by science and technology and that its members, particularly the young, look to the church for help in understanding this reality in the context of faith.

5. The church in the Western world needs to learn to listen to persons in the Third World, not asking how Third World ideas fit into the traditional First World ways of thinking but asking how Third World experiences with science and technology challenge the thinking and practices of the First World.

6. The church needs to consider appropriate ways to communicate with persons of varying levels of understanding, from intellectuals to the average people in the pew.

7. The church needs to be imaginative in finding ways to relate to existing institutions and groups that address science and technology (for instance, colleges and universities, schools, professional groups, community action groups).

8. Perhaps most important of all, the church must take initiatives to see that its future clergy are educated for the age of science and technology in which they will minister.

◆ RECOMMENDATIONS ◆

The international roundtable recommended that:

1. The Evangelical Lutheran Church in America and the Lutheran World Federation appoint a continuation committee whose responsibilities would be:
    a. to draft a proposal for funding from church bodies and foundations
    b. to appoint, for a two-year term, a coordinator for a new international roundtable. The functions of the coordinator would be:
        (1) to create a survey of existing groups and activities
        (2) to test the feasibility of fitting proposed work into the programs of existing centers and institutes
        (3) to seek ongoing funding from church judicatories and foundations for continuing work of the roundtable after the two-year period
        (4) to promote the work of the roundtable among international church judicatories
        (5) to encourage the educational and pastoral networking goals within local church bodies
        (6) to appoint an international roundtable on science, religion, and society with membership to include both young and experienced scientists and theologians, social scientists, women, and church leaders. Members should come from both Western and Third World nations.
2. The international roundtable develop its work with two emphases:
    a. Science and theology discussion (the theoretical issues of epistemology, methodology, and language), including:
        (1) identification of issues to be developed
        (2) creation of support functions for various networks engaged in the dialogue such as theologians, ethicists, scientists, pastors, chaplains, and educators
        (3) initiation of educational programs for seminary professors and pastors, including educational materials for use in parishes
    b. Public expression on social issues, perhaps through the creation of a forum with representatives from international ecumenical bodies (e.g., World Council of Churches, World Student Christian Federation), world confessional bodies (e.g., Lutheran World Federation), Christians from the social sciences, national church leaders, theologians, ethicists, and lay persons in politics and economic and social affairs.

The functions of the forum would be:

● to review world science-technology developments and suggest issues for the churches' consideration and action;

● to convene such international meetings or conferences as would encourage world Christian cooperation on particular issues;

● to encourage seminars on issues of regional concern, especially in regions where financial resources are lacking for such purposes;

● to maintain close contact with international agencies that are working on issues of science and technology;

● to publish and circulate information about the experience of local and national churches and Christian groups dealing with these problems;

● to work with those promoting dialogue with other living faiths on issues of science and technology.

The following are examples of the types of problems to be addressed:

● military weapons and human survival (nuclear, biochemistry, Star Wars)

● Third World ecological problems and agricultural "development" (use of local technology)

● genetic engineering (human and agricultural)

● industrial technological development and the consequences for the environment (chemical industrial waste, ecological problems)

● AIDS

● medical ethics

♦ CURRENT WORK IN SCIENCE AND THEOLOGY ♦

Without presuming to have access to complete information on existing work in science and theology, the roundtable did share the following activities in which its members were involved.

Academies, Institutes, and Centers

Evangeliche Akademie Lochum, Federal Republic of Germany:
With a staff of three theologians and seven scholars from other disciplines, the academy provides programs and conferences for pastors and laity in a variety of issues, including science and theology. The intention is to approach issues in a comprehensive manner. A focus on ecological issues, for example, will include discussion of the theoretical issues of science and theology, the philosophy of nature, and technological policy.

Ian Ramsey Centre, St. Cross, Oxford University, England:
The center was established to address the ethical problems generated by science and technology from a philosophical and theological point of view. It now works with a forum of 200 persons, meeting annually to discuss issues of science and theology. The center participated in the First European Conference on Science and Religion in 1985 and now shares in the planning of the second conference, which is expected to lead to a more established structure for continuing the discussions in Europe.

Institute for Ethics and Philosophy and Religion, University of Aarhus, Denmark: The institute has been established within the university for purposes of fostering dialogue among scientists and theologians. It hosted the First European Conference on Science and Religion, the papers from which will be published under the title, *Free Will and Determinism.*

Center for Theology and the Natural Sciences, Berkeley, California, USA: The purpose of CTNS is to sponsor research and teaching in theology and the natural sciences, with emphasis on cosmology, physics, biology, philosophy of science and of religion, and historical issues in religion and science. An affiliate of the Graduate Theological Union, CTNS sponsors seminary and doctoral courses, awards an annual fellowship to an outstanding scholar for research and teaching, convenes national and international conferences, holds public forums, and offers church workshops. Included are scientists, clergy, technologists, university and seminary faculty, students, and the general public. Over 350 CTNS members receive the quarterly *CTNS Bulletin* and bi-monthly *CTNS Newsletter.*

Center for Religion and Science, Lutheran School of Theology in Chicago, USA: The center, now in the process of development, will focus on such issues as: 1) how we understand the world and our place in that world; 2) how the traditional concerns and beliefs of religion can be related to scientific understanding; and 3) how the joint reflection of scientists, theologians, and others can contribute to the welfare of the human community.

Through research, teaching, and outreach programs, the center will be a place where scientists, theologians, and other scholars will collaborate on interpreting classic Christian theology in ways that communicate in the context of contemporary scientific understandings. Colloquia, seminars, conferences, and continuing education programs will be offered.

Center for Theological Inquiry, Princeton, New Jersey, USA: The center was created as a place for scholars to be in residence for a specified period of time to do research, writing, and collaboration with other scholars. The focus of the program depends on the fields of interest of the scholars in residence. The present fields are science and theology, ethics, and the history of theology.

Trinity Institute, New York, USA: The institute provides a means for theological renewal and continuing education for clergy of the Episcopal Church. It holds regional and national conferences; those in 1986 focused on science and theology. In the last year, the institute has taken the initiative in identifying fifty priests with doctorates in the natural sciences. In cooperation with the Center for Theology and the Natural Sciences, Berkeley, a conference is being planned for these priests, with the expectation that a network will be formed to include these priests plus Episcopal lay persons who are scientists.

Church Bodies

Moving from the activity of centers, institutes, and academies to that of church bodies, the general observation was that the fundamental problem in getting science and theology issues raised with any continuing seriousness within the churches has been due to the failure to lodge the responsibility and to provide staff and funds for the enterprise. Some initiatives, however, were reported to the roundtable.

The Presbyterian Church USA has had a "Theology and Cosmology" group, established to foster an analysis and discussion of science and theology. The group was responsible for a paper, "The Dialogue between Theology and Science," which was adopted by the General Assembly of the Presbyterian Church USA and commended for study to the congregations and seminaries. The paper included sections on theology and science, biblical perceptions and scientific developments, the background for the dialogue between theology and science, the development and promise of post-Newtonian science, and the restrictions of finitude. The Presbyterian Church USA is one of the denominations that participate in United Ministries in Education, which will be discussed later.

The United Church of Christ, USA is in the earliest stages of planning an ongoing program in science and technology. Its primary work has been in the area of genetic engineering, on which a pronouncement is being prepared for submission to the 1989 General Synod. As with most of the other denominations, the United Church has developed official policies on particular issues raised by science and technology, for example, environmental and ecological issues, and nuclear and bio-chemical weaponry. The United Church is also a participant in United Ministries in Education.

The Lutheran Church in America is one church body that does have science and theology on its agenda. The Division for World Mission and Ecumenism was largely responsible for the conference in Cyprus. In addition, its Division for Mission in North America has held Faith and Life Institutes on issues of science and theology. These institutes are generated by laity and focus on issues selected by the laity.

The Evangelical Lutheran Church in America's Division for Global Mission has as an objective in the life of this new church body a discussion of the nature of mission in the context of the realities of contemporary culture. How is the mission of the church to be articulated in a scientific-technological world? The priorities of the new division are:

1. Articulating the meaning of the gospel amidst cultures of the world by working with Christian communities around the world, including the scientific communities.

2. Dealing with development issues in fifty countries, including assisting people to be aware of their own values, especially as they face questions of the appropriate use of technology.

3. Concern with justice issues, particularly in South Africa, the Middle East, and Central America.

4. Attention to peace issues, including the use of nuclear and chemical weaponry.

5. Educating the Lutheran constituency regarding the human situation, including education about hunger, oppression, and nuclear war issues.

Since ninety-two percent of the people in Denmark are members of the Lutheran Church, it is difficult to determine "the work of the church" in the public arena. Parliament has formed an ethics committee to articulate guidelines for research in science and technology. Members of the committee are members of the church.

Church initiatives by the Lutheran Church in Sweden are now leading to the development of courses and conferences that will focus on environmental, ecological, and peace issues. This is partly in response to Chernobyl, which had disastrous effects on the sea waters (killing and poisoning the fish), forests, and animal life, especially in Lapland. As in other churches, the pastors have little background in science and technology and thus feel uncomfortable entering discussions on the subject.

The Church of England's Board of Social Responsibility has produced a series of distinguished reports dealing with the various issues raised by science and technology. It is frequently asked to provide assistance to government commissions charged with addressing specific issues raised by the uses of science and technology. Strong initiatives are being made to place science and technology on the agenda of the Lambeth Conference in 1988.

The Archbishop of York has formed a new order for priests who are also scientists. It is expected that the devotional rule of the order will lead to the development of new literature using theological expressions that are plausible to scientists.

The Evangeliche Kirche in Baden, Federal Republic of Germany, has been addressing the theoretical aspects of theology and science since the 1950s. A dramatic change in the level of attention to ethical issues of technology occurred after the Chernobyl disaster, which poisoned the air and contaminated fruits and vegetables in sections of Germany. Now issues of nuclear energy are viewed in terms of the effect on the environment.

The church has established a Commission for Environmental Concerns with an agenda: (1) to give church leaders, including pastors, good information about environmental and ecological issues; (2) to foster discussions on theology of creation; (3) to hold programs on ecology in the churches, encouraging a change of life-style, especially with regard to the use of energy; and (4) to provide speakers in the political arena for addressing environmental problems.

The Orthodox Syrian Church of the East in India is engaged in a historical investigation of science and technology as the product of the European Enlightenment. Metropolitan Paulos Mar Gregorios's book, *Enlightenment: East and West,* discusses the structures of the European Enlightenment and the enlightenment of Buddha.

A second consideration of the church focuses on the imbalance in the framework of the contemporary secular political and economic world, which views the universe as self-contained, thus eliminating such other considerations as the religious. A third area of work has been in medical education, with the aim of replacing the notion of the body as a machine with one that sees body, soul, and mind as one system requiring a holistic approach.

The World Council of Churches in 1975 issued a study entitled "Focusing Up to Nuclear Power" that generated considerable discussion in member churches. In 1979 the council sponsored its international Conference on Faith, Science, and the Future at the Massachusetts Institute of Technology (MIT). The common judgment about the failure of the MIT conference to have more follow-up was that there were inadequate clues about how to proceed with the agenda in the churches. They did not have places in which to lodge the concern nor persons in the structures who would take leadership in finding funds for program development.

In 1981 the council generated two studies, one on genetic engineering and the other on the use of nuclear weapons. The present program on justice, peace, and the environment has its focus on the use of science and technology for war and profit.

With the exception of factors concerning development, the Lutheran World Federation does not have science and technology on its agenda. An interest in issues raised by the use of electronic media and by the need for a new theology of creation seems to be emerging.

The Roman Catholic Church, under a papal commission, called a conference of twenty Protestant and Roman Catholic scholars at the Vatican Observatory in 1987. The aim was to begin a reconciliation of the church with science and scientists, especially in regard to epistemological and methodological issues. Included in the discussions were the doctrine of creation and a critique of contemporary natural theology.

United Ministries in Education, (UME) an ecumenical structure formed by six denominations in the United States, has been instrumental in fostering programs in medical education. Its purpose is to address issues of human values raised in the teaching, research, and practice of medicine. The program has led to creating faculties in the humanities in medical schools, with their teaching integrated into the regular curriculum of the schools. Such programs are now being extended into residency programs, schools of nursing, schools of dentistry, and other allied health institutions. The faculties include persons in the disciplines of theological and philosophical ethics, the history of science, and literature.

This activity has led to the formation of the Society for Health and Human Values with a membership of 600 persons, including many from the medical sciences, the social sciences, theology, and philosophy, among others. The society holds regional conferences and publishes resource materials. Its annual meeting is held in conjunction with the American Association of Medical Colleges, for which the society provides seminars and workshops on topics addressing value questions raised by new science and technology.

United Ministries in Education also sponsors a Program on Science, Technology, and the Christian Faith. The aim is to foster discussion in colleges and universities on topics of science and religion. The program is establishing ties with a concurrent movement on Science, Technology, and Society centered at Pennsylvania State University.

Seminaries

Throughout the conference in Cyprus a recurring theme was heard: The churches will not be significantly engaged in issues of science and theology until its clergy have been prepared to deal with the issues. Without presuming to have a complete survey of the seminaries in which science is a part of the curriculum, the roundtable noted the following resources:

Pacific Lutheran Theological Seminary, Berkeley, California, in the teaching of Professor Ted Peters.

The Graduate Theological Union, Berkeley, California, through the teaching of Professor Robert Russell and the courses and conferences of the Center for Theology and the Natural Sciences.

The Lutheran School of Theology at Chicago, through the teaching of Professor Philip Hefner and the offerings of the newly formed Center for Religion and Science.

The Louisville Presbyterian Seminary, Louisville, Kentucky, in the teaching of Professor Harold Nebelsick.

The Memphis Theological Seminary, Memphis, Tennessee, in the teaching of Professor Ronald Cole-Turner.

Universities

The international roundtable also noted activity at a number of educational institutions. At the University of Uppsala a group of professors in the sciences has formed to address ethical issues raised by science. On the basis of their discussions, a code of ethics has been developed to help individual scientists determine what research they should and should not do from the standpoint of their moral convictions. The code has been discussed throughout the universities of Sweden, resulting in some scientists' having changed their activities. The code asks scientists to support those who cease their research as the result of accepting the code of ethics.

The same group of scientists has begun to develop programs through which graduate students are expected to address ethical issues raised in and through their study and research. The group is now planning a conference for teachers with the aim of helping them address ethical issues raised in science and technology.

·B·

Africa

Deborah Enilo Ajakaiye

Definitions of science abound. A popular but rather simple one is that it is "a systematic study of nature" that is distinct from "technology" or the "tools of science."

Alternatively, science may be defined as the discovery of phenomena and laws of nature that have always existed but were unknown to humans, whereas technology refers to the creation of new products and processes and their application.

In the African context the distinction between science and technology is not so apparent. The perception of science by the general populace is influenced by its application in fields such as modern medicine, agriculture, and engineering. Science is often associated with products such as cars, planes, radios, television, sophisticated medical equipment, tractors, and weapons. A cross-section of the people in the rural areas, who form about eighty percent of the population, find it difficult to distinguish between science and magic.

Without belittling the intelligence of this class of people, we note that they are understandably unfamiliar with the rigorous scientific methodology involving the systematic collection and interpretation of data. This is because they have little or no formal scientific education or training.

On the other hand, school children—particularly those who have been through secondary school—have a better understanding of science. They regard it as useful, prestigious, and lucrative careerwise.

The intelligentsia in Africa fall into two categories, each with its own perception of science. One category consists of those not engaged in natural science, such as lawyers, poets, writers, and professional administrators. In the other category are natural scientists. The nonscientists in many countries appear not to take indigenous scientists and their scientific activities as seriously as they should. For instance, to carry out local projects they prefer to hire foreign (European/North American) scientists/technologists in preference to even more competent indigenous ones. Consequently the development of scientific initiative is inhibited. The perception of science by this class of people, including policy makers, is ambiguous and suspicious. They

144

realize the usefulness of science and technology to developmental needs but dare not encourage local initiatives so as to defend their stratum within the society. This attitude is greatly influenced by foreign interests who see indigenous technocrats as competitors and a threat to their hegemony.

Africa scientists recognize and appreciate the importance and impact of science in society. However, they are frustrated for lack of appropriate tools, resources, and encouragement to carry out their profession efficiently.

Church leaders, even though aware of the usefulness of the tools of science, appear to be disinterested in science policy issues. They give the impression that the acquisition of much scientific knowledge is anti-Christian. Such an attitude may be explained by the fact that the clergy (mostly Protestant) are usually not well versed in scientific matters.

Generally, though for very different reasons, there seems to be a collusion of silence between the political and religious leaders as to what science can do for the ordinary people. They have not taken the pains to explain the impact of science and technology to the masses they lead. If there appears to be an estrangement between religious leaders and scientists, it is probably not because of the antagonism and dichotomy that apparently exist between religion and science in the Western world. This is because in the African tradition there is no distinction between the sacred and the secular: God, humans, and nature are inextricable. African traditional values therefore enrich our perception of science and technology.

♦ PRESSING ISSUES ♦

Current pressing issues in Africa that are significantly influenced by science are health, food, shelter, and liberty. All aspects of developmental issues affecting these areas postulate the use of science. Unfortunately people think of science and technology as what is to come from overseas. But the examples of the U.S., Japan, and Korea show that successful application of science and technology to developmental needs must depend on indigenous know-how and capability.

The message for Africa is clear. If we must use science and technology for our development, we need to acquire, master, and adapt it to our needs. Some key points follow:

1. Blind and unjust importation of irrelevant and inappropriate technology has made several African nations poorer. Africa is one of the richest continents in terms of natural resources, as affirmed by African leaders themselves in the Lagos Plan of Action of 1980. Surprisingly, as we approach the end of the decade, Africa is poorer due to the exploitation of these resources by predominantly foreign companies using highly sophisticated scientific and technological tools.

Issues in which science itself is a controversial or urgent matter include misuse of computers for oppression through surveillance. For example, in Namibia and South Africa computerized ID's give vital information on individual racial, economic, social, and residential grouping.

2. The development of nuclear weapons by South Africa is a matter for concern by most African countries.

3. Arms importation in Africa encourages the perpetuation of wars and the devastation caused by wars. These wars lead to mass displacement of people and disruption of agricultural production that, in turn, often result in famine, disease, and death.

4. The promotion of contraceptive devices under the notion of "family planning" has led to the erosion of the sanctity of the African family. The African woman appears to be brainwashed into discarding the virtues of motherhood.

5. The AIDS question is also a controversial issue, since it is being presented in the Western press as originating from Africa. There is, however, no incontrovertible evidence as to the African origin of the AIDS virus. For if AIDS had indeed originated in Africa, it would have reached epidemic proportions long before now, given the poor health facilities of most African countries. Also, since the machinery for screening the AIDS virus is not controlled by Africans, the risks of distortion and manipulation of facts for political and economic interests cannot be excluded. For example, earlier statistical estimates of AIDS test results from some African countries have been proven to be inflated by subsequent, more precise tests. These more accurate estimates have, however, not been given the prominence earlier results enjoyed. Thus the current AIDS debate is considered by Africans as a resurgence of racism.

◆ AFRICA'S INHERITED CHRISTIAN FAITH ◆

Christianity was introduced into Africa (except Ethiopia) in the high colonial era by missionaries representing different denominations such as Roman Catholic, Baptist, Lutheran, Anglican, and the Apostolics. Out of these have now grown numerous African indigenous and independent churches and sects. As a result of this heritage, particularized traditions and theological expressions associated with these denominations in the Western world have been transplanted to the African scene.

The introduction of modern science into Africa was pioneered by these Western denominations mainly through the establishment of secondary grammar schools. The weakness of the relation of the inherited Christian faith to the impact of science was due first to the limited nature both of the education the missionaries themselves had and the scope of the scientific knowledge they were ready to dish out to Africans. This missionary attitude was an apparent complicity with the colonial authorities not to accord the Africans any high degree of scientific and technological formation. This fragmentation of the Christian front with their inherent financial limitations prevented the churches from establishing institutes of higher scientific learning. The consequence is that the contemporary scientific elite do not usually have a strong intellectual linkage with the Christian faith.

◆ CHRISTIAN WITNESS IN A SCIENTIFIC AGE ◆

In order for the church in Africa to communicate its faith with increased pertinence to science and to the influence of science in a way that fosters engagement and genuine Christian witness, she must focus on certain strategies.

Education of the clergy. The training of catechists, pastors, and other clergy should be intensified and broadened to include some scientific orientation, to equip them for ministry in an era in which the laity are becoming more highly educated.

Education of the laity. Several churches in Africa currently tend to limit rigorous biblical teaching to catechumen candidates, neglecting continuing adult Christian education. This attitude has resulted in the alienation of the elites, quite a number of which are scientists. Obviously to reverse this trend churches need to revive and intensify biblical teachings and prayer meetings among the laity.

A genuine effort also has to be made by the clergy to minister to and encourage this group of people.

Prophetic ministry of the church. The church has to be true to its prophetic calling. A lot of oppression and injustice presently exist in Africa, which the church must address through its public proclamation, fostering peace, justice, and freedom on the continent.

Use of modern technology. The peculiar needs of churches in Africa call for greater use of modern technological devices, such as radio, television, video, and film, for the propagation of the gospel.

◆ STRATEGY FOR THE CHURCHES IN AFRICA ◆

Some of the strategies the church in Africa should adopt over the next ten years in continuing a confrontation with the issues discussed above include the following:

1. Ecumenical dialogue between church leaders and intellectuals in the church should be initiated and sustained.

2. Churches should avail themselves of their infrastructures to increase the awareness of members of their congregations about issues of science and technology affecting their daily lives (for example, in public health delivery, environmental care, and community development).

3. Churches should take a prophetic stand against injustice generated both internally and externally (for example, apartheid in South Africa, violation of human rights, bribery and corruption, and manipulation of science and technology as instruments of oppression).

4. Education of clergy and other church leaders should be enhanced. Curriculum should be broadened, as discussed above, to incorporate some science and technology orientation with the necessary ethical and sociological contents to ensure a just, participatory society. This will also ensure better interaction with intellectuals in the churches.

5. Churches are hierarchical and exclusive in their present structures and practices. It is recommended that they become more participatory and inclusive.

6. Churches should have a program of continuing education for the laity, including the intellectuals and professionals within the church.

7. Churches will become richer if they utilize more rationally—for various projects—the professionals within their parishes.

8. There should be ecumenical consultations at national and regional levels to discuss the issues of science, technology, and theology. It is thus recommended that African churches should organize such conferences on a Pan-African level.

Participants' contributions to the implementation of the above recommendations could be twofold. Each participant should both undertake to introduce the recommendations to his or her home church, and endeavor to act as a resource person to promote the dialogue on science, technology, and theology in our various churches in Africa.

As a group, participants from Africa have initiated an "African Christian Intellectuals' Fellowship" (ACIF), whose main objective is to provide a forum for African Christian intellectuals willing and committed to bring their knowledge to bear on science, technology, and theological issues.

◆ C ◆

Asia

Pradip Thomas

The Asian continent is home to a bewildering array of races, ethnic divisions, and religious groups. It has been a fertile breeding ground for most of the world's great religions and has rich philosophical traditions, the accumulated wisdom of centuries, and a colorful cultural heritage.

Beginning with the era of colonialism, however, traditional cultures and world views were systematically devalued. The ideology and practice of "modernization" led to a process of economic and cultural substitution. Under the onslaught of modernization, most Asian countries promoted models of development incongruent with their past experiences and present needs. In a sense the dilemma of most Asian countries has been to reconcile the adaptation of Western science and technology to fit the cultural patterns of their people. Not many countries have succeeded, with Japan being the significant exception. Perhaps the greatest threat to Asian countries under the influence of modernization is a loss to both their individual and collective identities.

Contemporary Asian societies are at different stages of social and economic development. On the one hand there are industrial giants such as Japan and emerging giants such as South Korea. On the other hand there are countries such as India and Pakistan. Despite significant advances in the fields of science and technology, they are still grappling with basic problems of existence, including large-scale poverty, ignorance, and disease. There are also transitional societies such as Malaysia in which the conflict between continuity and change has led to all sorts of social and cultural problems.

In most parts of Asia, Christianity and Western science and technology were introduced under the aegis of colonialism: The missionary played a decisive role in the introduction and dissemination of Western science and technology. The world view spread by these missionaries was a dualistic one stressing the separation of humankind from nature and tending to be "otherworldly" in its orientation.

Both formal and informal systems of education promoted by Christian missions introduced rational systems of thought, the ideal of democracy, and the goal of equal opportunity. But they also led to a situation in which non-Western world views were excluded or devalued as subjects worthy of study. In post-independent Asia this trend has become so dominant that a number of societies are faced with cultural crisis. There is therefore a real need to evolve world views and systems of production that are in harmony with indigenous cultural needs.

Oriental religions such as Hinduism and Taoism are based on world views that see the created order as an indissoluble whole. Humanity is not conceived of in terms of its unique place within the order of the universe but in terms of its mutually symbiotic relationship with nature and with God. Reality is conceptualized in terms of a series of relationships that may be indeterminate but that consist of parts that are crucially linked to each other. Reality is seen as a whole, in terms of its various interrelationships, and not in terms of distinctive parts that can be independently measured and studied.

Unlike the Western scientific world view that emphasized the differences between faith and science, subject and object, nature and human, the Eastern world view stressed their interrelationships. Nature in the Newtonian world view was a given that could be subdued and dominated since nature was placed below human beings in the natural order.

In a number of subtle and significant ways, the post-modern scientific world view is closely related to some of the world views of the Eastern religions. The Hindu world view, for example, is in basic agreement with the discoveries made in the new physics, including the indeterminate nature of time and space and the relativity of matter. There is also a corresponding belief between post-modern scientific discoveries and Eastern religions that at the "heart of reality there lies an unfathomable mystery."

Post-modern science has exploded the comfortable myths of older scientific world views. It has shown that there may be questions to which there may not be clear or concrete answers. It has shown that the earth's resources are finite and that many of these resources are nonrenewable.

The effects of modernization in Asia have been devastating. Eco-systems have collapsed. There has been large scale environmental destruction, deforestation, pollution, and threat of lasting damage to humankind and nature posed by the dumping of nuclear waste in the seas and rivers. The Green Revolution has led to unanticipated consequences such as an increase in the gap between the rich and the poor and to the degradation of the environment due to the indiscriminate use of pesticides and fertilizers. Organic methods of cultivation, using locally available resources and letting land recuperate for itself by leaving it fallow, are devalued and seldom used. Although in the last twenty years the myths of modernization have been exposed, both the leaders and the intelligentsia in most Asian countries are still mesmerized by the prospect of increased productivity leading to better standards of living through modernization.

The sad truth is that the church in Asia is for all practical purposes still Western in orientation and supports the practice of modernization. Despite the fact that liturgies have been translated into local languages, they still do not reflect Asian culture. The source of the alienation of the Asian church lies in its inability to reconcile itself with the culture and living traditions of Asia.

Central to Christianity is the death-resurrection mystery of the Lord. From Vedic times there has been a primordial intuition foreshadowing the

Paschal mystery. According to Hindu tradition, at the heart of the universe—in the womb of the earth—is the altar of sacrifice where God is dismembered. From this dismemberment comes life for the world. This life-death cycle has vibrated through nature, where it is lived out annually in the seasons, and humankind is caught up in its salvific power. The use of science and technology in Asia has to be integrated into this life-death cycle that, in turn, inserts us into the Christian mystery of redemption.

Science and technology in theory and application in Asia have to be brought within the context of the mystery of religion, in which humankind expresses a close affinity with nature, not as an environment to be conquered and dominated, but as one to be befriended. Holding humankind and nature together is the all-pervasive presence of God as the loving Father, and this fatherhood of God is expressed in the kinship of humankind. It is into this framework that science and technology in Asia need to enter, not to dominate or manipulate, but to work with the people of Asia in the context of their needs and aspirations.

Apart from adapting the gospel message and contextualizing its meaning, the church in Asia needs to take a clear stand on moral and ethical issues related to developments in science and technology and to justice and human rights. Genetic engineering, for example, poses substantial moral and ethical problems. Amniocentesis, if introduced into societies in which women have traditionally been assigned a lower place than men, may be used to detect the sex of the unborn child, and if it is found to be female, may lead to its abortion. *In vitro* fertilization, the technique that has led to the phenomenon of test-tube babies and surrogate mothers, can pose various social and psychological problems to a child who has been conceived in such a way. Although the church has to value a person's freedom of choice, it must also take an active role in guiding people towards right choices regarding the use of advanced techniques of medical engineering.

The church in Asia is directly and indirectly involved in education at the primary, secondary, and tertiary levels. It is in a position to provide moral guidance and to disseminate relevant information on ethical issues related to developments in post-modern science and technology. Its educational services must be open to people of all castes, classes, and creeds. It must initiate a dialogue with scientists and technologists and at the same time take a firm stand on the importance of scientists' and technologists' following a code of ethics in their research and its applications.

Concerned social activists all over Asia have already initiated grassroots movements aimed at curbing the ceaseless exploitation of both the human being and nature by multinational corporations, the nuclear industry, the timber industry, the pharmaceutical industry, the advertising industry, and the knowledge industry in general.

The "people's science movements" that have sprung up all over India have had some success in popularizing a people's science, making available access to appropriate technology and helping scientists realize the importance of working with people in an effort to solve their own basic problems. Local systems of medicine have been popularized by a number of these groups. In the case of Malaysia, a cartoon strip has been used to promote the value of indigenous systems of medicine. The Christian hospital movement in Malaysia has deepened the Christian vocation of caring for the sick and the terminally ill.

Creative pedagogical methods have been devised in India based on the real needs of the people. More than twelve Christian colleges in Ranchi District, Bihar, have used a system of learning based on a philosophy and practice of tribal culture that emphasizes the essential unity of the created universe and the unity of human beings with the created order. In Japan, environmental groups have protested the dumping of radioactive material in the sea by Japanese companies. A number of groups and concerned people in Asia have tried, one way or another, to devise methods of development that are ecologically sound and related to the fulfillment of the real needs of the people. The church therefore needs to look at and learn from the experiences of these various social activist groups, involve them in the church's development programs, and also evolve people-based programs.

The church in Asia must assume a prophetic role in society. It needs to evolve an authentic Asian identity and a relevant Asian theology in the light of the reality of Asian societies.

In the light of Asian realities, the group recommends that:

1. The church in Asia should hold dialogues with scientists in Asia and urge them to adopt a code of ethics to govern their research and its applications.

2. The church in Asia should learn from the many social action groups in Asia who have planned, implemented, and evaluated a variety of models of effective grassroots development.

3. The church in Asia should play a prophetic role in society. There needs to be a revision in theological curricula in various seminaries, including provision for options on science and faith and the study of a specifically Asian theology of liberation.

4. Both pastors and members of the congregations should be made aware of emerging developments in science and technology and alerted to their various moral and ethical implications. Pastors should incorporate a more holistic and contextual world view to their homilies and sermons.

5. The church in Asia should try to devise regionally or locally specific liturgies that reflect the codes of local culture.

6. The church should make creative and innovative use of both "small" and "big" media. The wall paper, for example, can be used to spread relevant information on church-related and local realities.

7. The church in Asia should try to form networks of concerned Christians in their respective countries. These people can play an important role in advising members of the public who ask for advice on new developments in medicine, family planning, and the application of new technologies and developments in science.

At a more personal level, the Asian delegates plan to discuss these issues with friends, co-workers, and church members. We hope to support and encourage each other through an informal network.

·D·

Europe

♦ SUMMARY OF THEORETICAL DISCUSSIONS ♦

Sigurd Martin Daecke
Translated by Helmut T. Lehmann

Cyprus is on the way from Jerusalem to Athens. Even before the Apostle Paul reached Athens on his first missionary journey, he brought the Christian faith to Cyprus, a country defined by hellenistic philosophy and science. Consequently, at this conference the well-known question of the church father Tertullian has frequently been quoted, "What does Athens have to do with Jerusalem?" In other words, what does science have to do with faith?

The island of Cyprus itself became an icon of the relation between faith and science. Two hills dominating the skyline of Cyprus (Cyprian Olympus and Stavrovouni, on which there is a cloister) came to represent science and faith. Cyprus was well suited to illustrate that faith and science belong together.

Members of the European regional group (in which southern Europe was not represented) viewed those two hills, the Greek and the Christian, from the window of the room where their group met. They had little time, however, to listen to what the countryside and its history had to say to them, for the entire week at Larnaca was an encounter between natural science and faith: the natural scientists who at the same time were Christians and the theologians who were occupied with natural science. This encounter proved to be so difficult that for days on end more questions were raised than answers could be found, more problems were posed than solutions could be pointed out.

At the beginning the discussions were dominated by ethical questions dealing with the responsibility of natural scientists and technologists. The dangerous consequences of natural science and technology for human beings and nature, as well as the fateful commitments that result from the financing of research, were described.

Are we permitted to do everything we are able to do? This question was applied equally to the geneticist and to the atomic physicist, to electronics as well as to computer technology. Natural science and technology, it was decided, must recognize boundaries, inquire as to the results of their work for humanity and nature, and examine their presuppositions and their dependencies on government, the military, industry, and the economy.

The starting point of the discussion was the threat of natural science and technology for every human being and his or her health, for the exploitation of nature and the destruction of the environment. This was an

153

obvious place to begin because the "side effects" of technology are a part of the experience of the nonscientist.

The question as to whether natural science and technology should be permitted to do everything received a negative answer during the first part of the conversation dealing with ethical and ecological concerns. Clear boundaries were set for the freedom of research. Freedom of investigation must also be moral. Freedom in research must include the freedom to break off research. It must be freedom to refrain from insights and discoveries that can become harmful to humanity and nature. This view, for example, should be applied to both military and civilian atomic research, to the development of nuclear weapons and plants. And it is no less valid for gene technology and reproduction medicine.

The group, however, did not demand that natural science and technology stop research. Science and technology were not, as often occurs in discussions of this kind, condemned and disparaged in an impromptu way. We cannot escape from the scientific age and the technological/industrial society in which we live. We may not act, as some do today, as though that were possible. The fashionable overstatement of the criticism of science and technology is unrealistic and illusory.

In retrospect the group was grateful that a Swedish biologist and an English geneticist belonged to it. (On account of the latter the conversation of the Scandinavians and Germans could not be carried on in German, something which would have made it easier for some to express themselves. On the other hand, the salutary constraint to speak in English preserved the group from high philosophical flights, although attempts were made from time to time.) The natural scientists in the group prevented an ideological, impromptu critique. Time and again they called to mind that natural science and technology are not in themselves evil and harmful, not more sinful than many other things people do. They showed that natural science can also be applied in a good and helpful way and even that we urgently need them to overcome the evil consequences of exploitative and destructive technology (for example, to lower the consumption of energy and to protect the atmosphere, water, and food against pollution and poisoning).

At stake is only the kind of natural science and technology needed to preserve God's creation. Without scientists and technologists we cannot altogether carry out God's imperative to rule, the *dominium terrae*. If the human being is permitted to be God's co-worker, indeed even co-creator, as one of the lecturers suggested in connection with gene technology, then this task can only be carried out by means of a new and improved natural science and technology. And the more highly these are developed the more they can treat God's creation considerately.

When we dare (in genetic technology and reproduction medicine, for example) to apply the controversial concept of co-creator to the human being who either contributes to or hinders the realization of God's goals in creation with research and technology, then a judgment cannot be arrived at superficially. It can be determined only from case to case by means of a detailed scientific, environmental, and ethical discussion. Even then the ethical judgments will frequently remain controversial, as they may also within the church and theology.

In any case, it is important that natural scientists and technicians are aware of their responsibility before God for human life and for nature. The natural scientist can only do justice to this responsibility with a good conscience when exercising scientific competence of the highest order.

In the opinion of the group, these ethical and theoretical questions, the ontological problems, and the philosophy of science are closely related to each other in natural science and technology. How natural scientists and technicians deal with these questions and problems depends on what they believe. On the other hand, Christians, with their expectations of what natural scientists should do, get their bearings from how they understand natural science and technology.

Faith and understanding express themselves in language. So if the natural scientists and theologians want to understand each other, they must have a common language. Thus the discussion of questions in ethics and appropriate practice in our world was not in contradiction to the group's debate for almost a whole afternoon concerning the problem of language in the dialogue between the two communities: the scientific language of the scientific community and the religious language of the church's liturgy, doxology, and preaching.

Agreement, which was at stake in Larnaca between natural scientists and theologians, is only possible, then, when at least common structures of the languages spoken by both communities is present. And, with the aid of loan concepts from linguistic philosophy, these structures were found in the expressions "icon," "index," and "symbol." With these concepts the relationship can be described between reality—whether natural or religious—and the assertions concerning it by natural scientists and theologians. These concepts permit us to compare assertions concerning empirical experience and the experience of faith, for both the natural scientist and the theologian work with icons and symbols.

Though their justification was called into question within the group, these abstract and practical considerations served concrete and practical inquiries. Above all else at issue in the European group was a concern with how dialogue between natural scientists and theologians can be made possible and what their subject might be. Also at issue was the matter of education in the church so as to communicate information concerning the status of natural science today to co-workers, pastors, and congregations on the one hand, and, on the other hand, to communicate the theological implications of natural science.

Concerning the relationship between natural science and theology, many questions arose, prompted in part by the lectures. What consequences follow for theology, for example, from the world views of the theory of evolution and quantum theory? Must theology change its way of thinking and speaking? Is a change in paradigm necessary? What kind of a theology do we need to dialogue with natural scientists? Is there a theology specifically appropriate for natural scientists?

Models diametrically opposed to each other as presented (for example, by Nebelsick and Peacocke) in the morning lectures were the subject of debate. Are they to be reconciled with each other or must a person decide for one or the other? Are they alternative models? Is one of them *the* theology for the dialogue with natural scientists? One natural scientist in the group was of the opinion that most natural scientists do not want any theology at all because they feel they would thereby be "taken in." Is it appropriate for

Christian proclamation to natural scientists to try to make them Christians, perhaps even to make them ordained theologians? Or should mission not rather mean that theologians approach natural scientists without the intention of converting them so primary attention can be given to solving the world's problems, even with atheists. Instead of talking about God, should theologians not rather talk with scientists and technologists about nature and humanity so as to preserve these from destruction and annihilation?

But even if theologians do want to dialogue theologically concerning the meaning of natural science for faith and of faith for natural science, additional questions arise. Do natural scientists expect theologians to talk with them in their own language, perhaps the language of the theory of evolution or quantum theory or even of open systems? Should theologians interpret Christ and redemption, death and resurrection, in the context of evolutionary process? Or do natural scientists expect the theologian primarily to proclaim and interpret the biblical message without equivocation? Do they regard the understanding of God's relationship to natural reality as secondary to the faith preceding it? Should the assertions of faith and those of natural science merge into a harmonious world view, or do they lie on two completely different planes not touching one another? If they do not touch each other, is not the consciousness of the natural scientist who is a Christian split? Is not existence divided into two spheres, that of science and that of faith? If, on the other hand, the assertions of faith and science merge into a harmonious world view, is not the genuine nature of both surrendered in this synthesis? And yet in the understanding of the human being as co-creator, for example, it is necessary in the dialogue with gene technology to interpret God's creation as continuing creation *(cretio continua)* in the evolutionary process. Does the intellectual aspect get the short end of the stick in the case of the dualistic model, while the existential dimension comes up short in the synthetic model, for example, in questions concerning one's own guilt and death?

Here were questions and more questions, very different answers, and problems with no clearcut solutions. There was, however, unanimity concerning the fact that a theology for natural scientists must be clear and rationally comprehensible.

There was also a debate concerning which world view could become binding and serve as a basis for dialogue with natural scientists. Perhaps that of evolution or quantum mechanics? Do we have a modern or already postmodern world view? And who has which world view? Do we still more or less live with a Ptolemaic world view when we marvel at how beautifully the sun sets and fades into the sea? Does the world view of the scientist perhaps differ from that of a normal person, perhaps the theologian?

It was possible for the group to agree that different models of world views can exist side by side. But is dialogue with theologians thereby made more difficult or easier?

On the second afternoon a discussion concerning language was the presupposition for all these considerations. But not only the intellectual, rational aspect of the encounter between theology and natural science in the form of reflection, discussion, and information was at issue. Preaching in the church is a part of the process in the same way as is the church's educational task. Beside action and reflection, the ethical and theoretical dimension, there is in the church above all else the spiritual dimension. Does it perhaps remain as the only dimension that is unrelated and timeless alongside natural science and its world view? Is it still beholden to a world view of the past? The group asked itself how liturgy, doxology, and prayer can now encounter natural science and its world views. And how are they changed and shaped thereby?

These questions should not have been altogether surprising. Especially in the eucharist, the sacrament, faith already finds a close relationship between God and nature. It saw it even when the sacramental understanding of nature had a completely different way of viewing nature than the current objectifying and analyzing way of natural science. Could not the different views turn out otherwise in the future through the encounter of the spiritual and doxological dimension of the church with contemporary natural science? After all, sacramental thinking knows that God has accepted and sanctified nature in that he has through his incarnation entered it. And faith says that this nature, sanctified by his incarnation, is none other than the nature that is the object of the natural scientist's research. However, the question remains open as to how liturgy and doxology can now concretely confess this insight of faith.

In any case, for a real encounter between the Christian faith and natural science it is not sufficient merely to reflect on and debate this relationship and provide information concerning it— regardless of whether we insist on the model according to which thinking may only follow faith in the preceding Word of God, or on the other model, according to which natural scientific thinking shapes the expression of faith. It is not sufficient only to arrange for conferences and consultations, as important as this kind of encounter of natural scientists and theologians will be in the future.

All three problem areas debated by the group were judged as equally important: first, the ethical aspect; second, that of reflection and discussion; and third, the liturgical-doxological and eucharistic-sacramental aspect. Doing and speaking, confession, prayer, and sacrament must all take their place in the encounter between natural science and faith. A new spirituality made fruitful by the knowledge of natural science could enrich the spiritual life of the church. And also the eucharist, the gratitude of the church for its liberation and redemption through Jesus Christ, encompasses nature as experienced by natural scientists and matter as transformed by technicians.

♦ SUMMARY OF PRACTICAL DISCUSSIONS ♦

Rainer Stahl

All members of our group want to underscore their personal commitment to the questions with which we have dealt. We are giving thought to how to follow up on the conference in daily life.

We have stressed within our group the using of the already existing structures in our churches. Especially in the western part of Europe, we can strengthen the work of the ongoing scientific-religious dialogue and of the World Student Christian Federation. We recall the roundtable discussions in

West Germany out of which recommendations and study materials have been coming concerning genetics. These materials need to be implemented in a more direct way.

In eastern Europe, on the other hand, materials concerning possible activities in the field of scientific-theological discussion have not been available to the discussion in the conference. The integration of concerned people and institutions from churches in eastern Europe into a network of contacts needs special attention.

The group would like to mention the question of financing future work. Establishing some kind of network among the members of our group and integrating different activities will face us with this question. For the present, however, we want to thank the Lutheran Church in America and the Lutheran World Federation for initiating the discussion, exchange, and encounter in Cyprus.

Members of our group also identified several special tasks. Here the group would like to underscore the necessity of some scientific education of students of theology. Through such an education they would become aware of the urgent issues. It also should provide an overview and general understanding of the current trends in science. It should not just be burdened with detailed exercises in physics, biology, and the other sciences. In eastern Europe, such an education would also have the task of informing about additional philosophical interpretations of natural science than just the materialistic and atheistic one.

The organization of contacts with scientists on several levels will have special importance: On the level of the local parish it will be mainly a discussion with medical doctors, for example, about such questions as modern transplantation, or the possibility of prayer in the frame of a scientific world view. On the broader level is the necessity of pushing church leaders to become aware of the scientific/theological/technological/ethical issues. Especially in eastern Europe these issues have not been discussed with any frequency.

Finally we wish to stress the idea of building contacts in the frame of the traditional university. This is the place where theologians and scientists will get together most often.

The group emphasizes that preaching, education, and church activity should be shaped by questions of science and faith. This should be done in a way that takes up the real frontiers of church work: death, evil, resurrection. A kind of combination in tension has to be the aim. We have to proclaim the personal resurrection of each unique person—even the one who preaches—and also take into account the biological importance of death for all life. There the group thinks of a mutual influence between the way of thinking and speaking both of science by theology and of theology by science. Even if it sounds theoretical, the group was aware that this has to be carried out through an intellectual, a celebrating, and a practical way.

When our group considered content-related aims, it became clear that the first aim of our work should be to work on a satisfying expression of theology growing out of teamwork between theologians and scientists. In this connection the group had a long discussion on the problem of language. What does the sentence, "God acts," really mean? We found that science and theology have a similar situation concerning language pictures. Both need icons, symbols, and indexes that refer to different realities. Icons, symbols, and indexes are best developed if they open up a relatively broad horizon of association and understanding.

Secondly, we need a dialogue between the different world views within our societies. We have spoken about real science, alternative science, and the popular transforming of science. Each of these possibilities has an impact on society. The church needs to struggle with all of these aspects and to call for responsibility on all levels.

Thirdly, it is important to integrate the scientific and technological challenge into our liturgical life. In that connection it should be possible to elaborate prayers and creeds that offer formulations of our faith and that show the encounter with science and technology. Such material could lead to a deeper understanding of such common symbols, icons, and indexes as the elements in the eucharist.

Finally, the group wants to emphasize that all of this work has to be understood as a contribution to the mission of the church. There we think of a multidimensional missionary task. The activities are different for different groups in the church. Different problems and issues, and even different solutions to one problem, will occur. Our task is not so much to adapt the faith to new challenges as to grasp the faith implications of the more complete picture of the created order that scientists continue to bring.

·E·

Latin America

Vítor Westhelle

The uneven development of Latin American societies sets definite limits to an ideal encounter between world views of different intellectual communities. The problem is not so much one of confronting a North Atlantic approach with a Latin American one but of recognizing that certain social, cultural, political, and economic conditionings impose a different agenda.

Latin American countries are not underdeveloped so that they could be seen as trailing behind Europe or the U.S. in time. We have highly developed enclaves comparable to countries in the North. But at the same time, we have tribal people living nomadic lives. Four thousand years of world history co-exist within the boundaries of a single country. Any attempt to build bridges for dialogue that is oblivious to these social, historical, and cultural layers—which, in turn, have their corresponding world views—will be condemned to irrelevancy.

The challenge we face in our subcontinent is not just an ethical one. Our challenge demands serious consideration of what is at stake in an encounter of different ideologies and world views. If only a few strata or intellectual communities are involved in an encounter, the question is unavoidable: Whose interest is it to promote the world views of modern science?

In Latin America the mechanistic or Newtonian world view is not the main confrontational pole against the world picture of quantum physics. Quantum physics is not a challenge precisely because it has not set itself against the kaleidoscope of world view fragments scattered throughout the cultures of the continent.

♦ THE TECHNOLOGICAL INVASION ♦

An old saying that Brazilian folklore attributes to a Dutch colonizer of the seventeenth century asserts, "There is no sin south of the equator." This saying indeed expresses the daily experience of the Latin American people in regard to the impact of technology. The technological invasion is being carried out with ambiguous results.

160

There are cases in which advanced technology is used with exemplary ethical responsibility. A genetic databank works in Argentina to trace missing children and the remains of victims of the military dictatorship. Video technology is making an increasing impact in grassroot educational programs throughout the continent.

On the other side of the spectrum, however, we have indiscriminate use of pesticides in agriculture, lack of control over the drug industry in which unsafe products are sold and warnings about hazards are not issued, covert interests in the development or importation of nuclear technology, abusive use of electronic and computer technology for ideological surveillance, and genetic and biological experiments made without public control.

Technology is relatively accessible. But the means of controlling its use and application are not. Recently in Brazil, a junk dealer used a hammer to open a lead container that held isotope crystals of Cesium 137 used for cancer treatment. As a result, radiation seriously affected the lives of more than 100 persons, killing some of them. This tragic example of the nearness of technology and the distance of compatible knowledge brings to the agenda a challenge that needs to be addressed with utmost seriousness.

Latin America is a market for technological products, but it is not a partner in technological research. The decision of the Brazilian government to create a protected internal market for micro-computers has been conceived to foster the development of national technology in the field. For years, however, Brazil has been threatened with retaliatory measures by the U.S. government. Recently these threats turned into an official boycott of several Brazilian products exported to the U.S. market.

Although most of the technological gadgets that determine the lives of the people are produced in Latin American plants, the technological control belongs to transnational corporations based in Europe, the U.S., or Japan. That the research is done abroad only helps to increase the technology gap. Army laboratories do some research but primarily in the development of weapons (mostly conventional, but also nuclear in the cases of Argentina and Brazil). And there is hardly any feedback into civilian research.

♦ SCIENCE AND SOCIETY ♦

Technological gadgets are relatively accessible. The scientific knowledge that fosters and controls technology, however, as well as the theoretical achievements of advanced science, belong to another world. This situation has created an idealized view of science by the public. The good-scientist image is an ethereal incarnation of progress. Cultural traces of the long-range influence of the French Enlightenment's ideals and of nineteenth-century positivism remain as the ideological residue of a naive belief in progress. The picture of the good but irrelevant scientist will remain as long as there is little governmental support for scientific developments and as long as the corporations that mediate technological advance are foreign based.

The lack of support for scientific research has exiled scientists to university chairs where little research is done and almost no recognition is given. Labs are obsolete and lack equipment. The scientific community is isolated from international exchange and frequently lacks updated scientific information. To this picture must be added the brain drain, which is quite understandable but which definitely postpones the reversal of the trends.

The impact of a scientific world view is at most a marginal phenomenon. Lack of advanced and original research turns science into a warehouse of established information that is passed down through the educational system or the media, resulting in simple repetition of single experiments and in compartmentalized information.

It is impossible to speak of a world view that is characteristic of Latin American culture. There are not only regional differences. A pervasive syncretism issues from varied modes of experiencing a world quite unpredictable and unreliable in political, sociological, cultural, and economic terms. The high mobility and instability of the peoples of the continent (who experience political turmoil, displacement and migration, and economic oscillations) are at the root of the common syncretic ensembles of images, symbols, and views brought together without logical connections but with the function of anchoring psychological identity.

Bridges are being built by the social and human sciences. Through the social sciences, an organic integration between a scientific knowledge, alienated from the lives of the people, and the syncretic ensemble of images, symbols, and views is finding a tentative point of contact. It is impossible to conceive of the relevance of the modern scientific world view for Latin America if the social sciences are not invited as a mediating factor in this endeavor.

◆ THEOLOGY AND THE CHURCH ◆

The Latin American social sciences have taken the initiative in developing an integrated view of reality that overcomes syncretism yet maintains respect for the images, symbols, and views that people uphold. Latin American theology has followed this lead in the last two decades. It has sought to develop an indigenous theology that understands itself as a "second word" in reference to the "first word" coming from the social sciences. In this respect theology has been able to foster the organic commitment of the social sciences and of the church with the people. Several institutes and centers for documentation, analysis, and education have been created in the last fifteen years. Their goals are to integrate research in theology and in the social sciences and not only to inform but also to form and equip the peoples of Latin America so they can understand, interpret, and intervene consciously in the world in which they live. Here a true dialogue is going on.

There is indication that the natural sciences can also be integrated into this effort. There is no dichotomy between ethical and theoretical agendas. The social sciences have taught us that responsible ethical stances allow for relevant theoretical propositions. Signs of a growing integration of scientific fields in this project have already appeared. Recent research with medicinal herbs is recovering an almost lost popular pharmaceutical technology. It is also creating space for research in countries where the pharmaceutical industry is almost totally controlled by transnational corporations.

In this context the church has become a host for these efforts, notwithstanding institutional and confessional resistances. The awareness that this project must be undertaken has, to a large extent, prevailed in the church. The alternative is to become increasingly alienated in the midst of a process that is bringing about some results.

On another level, the church as long been involved in a science-theology dialogue. This communication happens within some segments of the middle class that have been historically challenged by secularization. Here we see similarities with the North Atlantic effort to relate science and theology as an encounter of fairly well-defined world views. In Latin America the efficacy of this effort has been weak, although it varies in different regions.

◆ FACING THE CHALLENGES ◆

The traditional and newly emerging challenges in Latin America do not allow for only a dialogue among people of good will in the scientific and theological communities and nothing more. The dialogue imposes itself from the very fact that science and technology are changing the lives of the people while simultaneously there is an increasing lack of control over these changes. Thus we suggest:

● that initiative be taken to establish a regional network of contacts among those who have been sensitive to the problem;

● that a steering committee be created to coordinate the work and challenge theologians and scientists to be ethically responsible in their theoretical endeavors;

● that an intentional interdisciplinary effort be made to foster a dialogue that will include the natural and the social sciences, theology, and other relevant religious and nonreligious world views;

● that institutes and centers for the joint work of scientists and theologians be motivated to implement such a program at various levels;

● that the churches be sensitized to this issue so as to be the space in which this venture can be further pursued;

● that ecumenical and missionary agencies be instrumental in pursuing and supporting these efforts; and

● that an international network with groups of similar concern be created, particularly among the continents of Africa, Asia, and Latin America.

◆F◆

North America

Eric C. Shafer

A fable tells of Buddha's holding a contest for men and women to design the most beautiful object. A woman designed a suspension bridge. It was very beautiful. Buddha rewarded her with all the gold she could carry away. A man designed a wall. Buddha rewarded him by sitting on him!

Building bridges instead of walls is an appropriate theme, not only for the entire conference, but also for the North America group reflection on the conference's topics. We quickly became aware that building bridges would not be easy for us as North Americans for three reasons:

First, our group did not represent North America. It contained voices from only the United States.

Second, our United States voices were hardly representative of our country or of the Evangelical Lutheran Church in America (ELCA). Eleven of our thirteen members were white males. None was from a minority group in our nation or church.

Third, many people in this world regard the United States as a major contributor to the problems involving science and technology. Included are such issues as the distribution of world resources for scientific investigation, the military control of scientific research, a long list of environmental concerns, and the genetic and medical issues in science.

Add to these the difficulty of communication between science and theology. This problem surfaced in our group when theologians felt left out of the discussion one day and scientists the next!

Let me quickly add that we have been able to build bridges of understanding among the members of the North America group. Our dialogue has led us to five recommendations:

First, we ask that the Evangelical Lutheran Church in America prepare a comprehensive study on the issue of "Christian Faith and the Scientific World." This study should include an interpretation of the Christian faith and tradition in light of the scientific and technological world in which we live. It should draw out the manifold and global implications science and technology have for Christian education, for new and varied worship forms, and for theological education.

164

Second, we call on the ELCA to foster congregational support of and sensitivity to the technologically influenced, not only those who work in technological areas but all of us who live in this increasingly technological society. We would hope that our congregations become communities of bold faith and honest doubt, with a special concern for the pastoral care of those whose work faces them with moral dilemmas related to military applications of technology.

Third, we look to the ELCA to provide curricular materials in the area of Christian education in a technological world. Attention needs to be directed to worship, Sunday school, catechetics, and the entire area of how this scientific/technological world affects our young people, from the earliest ages in our Christian education programs to their emergence as young adults in our Lutheran church colleges and campus ministries.

Fourth, we expect the ELCA to provide theological education for our pastors and associates in ministry that will prepare them for service in the twenty-first century. Faculty dialogues, continuing education opportunities, and synodical work with those preparing for lay and ordained occupations within the church are all situations in which the relationship between science and theology can be emphasized.

Fifth, we assume that the center for the study of science and theology at the Lutheran School of Theology in Chicago and at the Center for Theology and the Natural Sciences in Berkeley will be promoted and funded by the ELCA and that out of their ministry regional groups will be formed to bring scientists and technologists together with pastors and theologians for mutual support and dialogue.

These five recommendations are our major challenges to the ELCA. We have prepared preliminary strategies for carrying them out and, in many cases, thought of personnel who might be responsible for their implementation. We hope that the ELCA will not work in isolation on this topic but will approach it in an ecumenical fashion. We are ready to become a U.S. network on the subject and to invite others to join us. We plan to prepare common resolutions for presentation at synodical conventions across the U.S. in support of these recommendations. We envision some specific activities at and around the 1989 ELCA convention in Chicago. We hope to get on-line with existing computer networks throughout the nation. And our hopes even extend to the possibility of an ELCA television series on science and theology.

Whatever the results of our recommendations, we ask that the study and its resultant programs be done in relationship with U.S. corporations.

So many bridges to build. So many walls to break down.